This Is My Life

Other historical books published by
SOUTH WALTON THREE ARTS ALLIANCE, INC.

The Way We Were:
Recollections of South Walton Pioneers

Of Days Gone By:
Reflections of South Walton County, Florida

Seventy-Seven Years in Dixie:
The Boys in Gray of '61 - '65
by Henry William Reddick

This Is My Life
Beginning 1889 Through 1976

REVISED EDITION

By

Walker H. Reddick, Sr.

A publication of
COASTAL HERITAGE PRESERVATION FOUNDATION

A branch of
SOUTH WALTON THREE ARTS ALLIANCE, INC.
Santa Rosa Beach, Florida

This Is My Life: Beginning 1889 Through 1976 was published by the author, Walker H. Reddick, Sr., in 1977.

Copyright © 1986 by Walker Homer Reddick, Jr.

Revised and reprinted with permission from Walker Homer Reddick, Jr.

All rights reserved. No part of this publication may be reproduced, stored in a retrieval system or transmitted in any form by any means electronic, mechanical, photocopying, or otherwise, without first obtaining written permission of the copyright owner.

This revised edition was published in 2001 by
Coastal Heritage Preservation Foundation
A branch of
South Walton Three Arts Alliance, Inc.
P. O. Box 2042
Santa Rosa Beach, Florida 32459

Printed in the United States of America

ISBN# 0-9666805-3-7

Front cover photograph—Circa 1910
Walker H. Reddick, Sr. poses with Mrs. Florence Lewis (possibly a cousin) and her son in this picture postcard taken in Pensacola, Florida. Courtesy, Anne and W. Homer Reddick, Jr.

Oft in the stilly night,
Ere Slumber's chain has bound me,
Fond Memory brings the light
Of other days around me;
    The smiles, the tears,
    Of boyhood's years,
The words of love then spoken;
    The eyes that shone
    Now dimmed and gone,
The cheerful hearts now broken.

                – Thomas Moore
                National Airs

Autobiographer at Work

Walker H. Reddick, Sr.
Photo courtesy of
Thomasville (Georgia) *Times-Enterprise.*

Contents

Preface to Revised Edition ix

Foreword xi

Part I - Boyhood around the Choctawhatchee Bay

1. So Many Brothers and Sisters 3
2. Slow Horse Ride to School 9
   Choctawhatchee Bay around 1900 Map 10-11
3. First Train Ride 15
4. Sailing to Pensacola 20
5. Fun and Frolic at Oyster Lake 26
6. Hog Hunting near Devil's Swamp 32
7. Whale of a Tale 39
8. Father's Civil War Stories 47
9. Cowboy Days 55
10. Dangerous Journey to Ione's 59
11. The Wesleys and the Stricklands 65
12. Living the Bachelor's Life in Santa Rosa 72
13. 1905 Yellow Fever Outbreak 78
14. Oyster Dredging in Biloxi 85
15. Selling the Family Land 90

PART II - LIFE AS A RAILROAD MAN

 16. Telegraph Operator 101
  Some Early Railroad Routes of the
  Southeastern United States Map 108-109
 17. Wedding Bells 112
 18. Surviving the 1918 Influenza Epidemic 125
 19. Making Cairo Our Home 139
 20. Days of the Depression 149
 21. Attacked by a Cock-Fighting Rooster 158
 22. Visit to the Old Home Place 163

FAMILY GENEALOGY
  Reddick/O'Neal Family 173
  Henry W. Reddick's Siblings and Their Families 179
  The McCormick Family 182
  Reddick Cemetery 185
  Endnotes 187

SUGGESTED READING 189

Preface to Revised Edition

WHEN A FEW MEMBERS of the South Walton Three Arts Alliance began, in 1996, to research and write a history book about the southern part of Walton County, Florida, we came across two autobiographies by a father and son, who lived in our area in the 1800s and early 1900s and had the foresight to document their fascinating lives. Both books are a treasure to our local history, offering a glimpse into days long forgotten, and I vowed to get them back in print to share with future generations.

Self-published in 1910, Seventy-Seven Years in Dixie: The Boys in Gray of '61 - '65 was written by Henry William Reddick (1833-1924), recounting his life as a soldier in the First Florida Infantry during the American Civil War.

The second book, This Is My Life: Beginning 1889 Through 1976, was written by Henry's son, Walker H. Reddick, Sr. (1889-1981). Walker Reddick documents his hard-working yet blissful boyhood on the shore of Choctawhatchee Bay on the southwestern peninsula of Washington County, now a part of Walton County. The narrative continues with his career as a railroad man, working for six different railroads throughout the Southeastern United States. Mr. Reddick's folksy tone describes these events in vivid detail, with some memories reaching back eighty years.

Before tackling the job of republishing these two books, I contacted Walker Reddick's son, W. Homer Reddick, Jr., and his wife, Anne, who live in Macon, Georgia. Homer graciously granted me permission to edit and revise the memoirs written by his father and grandfather. (The revisions to Seventy-Seven Years in Dixie were completed in 1999 and it is in circulation again.)

According to Anne, Walker Reddick labored for several years, sitting at his manual typewriter for hours on end, writing his autobiography. "He had a good memory and felt he truly had something important to share," his daughter-in-law fondly recalls. "Mr. Reddick was so warm and friendly, always hugging everyone. He was a kind man who had great respect for all people—the perfect gentleman."

Upon the manuscript's completion in 1976, its typewritten pages were photocopied and bound, and the homemade book was handed out to relatives and friends. Walker Reddick's age was eighty-seven. He lived four more years after completing his narrative.

At the back of his book, Mr. Reddick included his family genealogy along with the listing of those buried at the small family cemetery—his grandmother, three brothers, and a few neighbors. The graveyard is still safely hidden in the piney woods west of Mack Bayou. Both lists have been included here.

This revised edition includes the photographs Walker Reddick used in his original publication, along with many others to illustrate some of the people, places, and events in his life. Two maps have also been included. The first is labeled Choctawhatchee Bay around 1900, and it shows the locations mentioned in the first part of this book, making easy reference for the reader. The second map, Some Early Railroad Routes of the Southeastern United States, corresponds with Mr. Reddick's travels and career with the railroad.

I have also added historical background on the Florida towns of Santa Rosa, St. Joseph, and Noma; Chattahoochee's Florida State Hospital; Apalachicola Northern Railroad; and two famous men from Apalachicola—Dr. John Gorrie and William Lee Popham.

A special thanks goes to Port St. Joe resident Billy Howell, who enthusiastically provided information and photographs of the Apalachicola Northern Railroad from his extensive collection. Beckie Buxton, historian of Freeport Archival Collection, deserves a large measure of gratitude for sharing pertinent historical data. I am grateful to Marilyn Schroer, Nancy James, and Mary Brockett, who served as copy editors. The generous help of the Reddick/O'Neal descendants contacted while searching for dates of births, marriages, and deaths, is also greatly appreciated.

– Karen Schansman
Editor
June 2001

Foreword

IT IS A PRIVILEGE and joy to share the experience of a lifetime recorded by Walker H. Reddick, Sr. in his documentary titled *This Is My Life*. It is the true story of his life beginning with the happiness and pleasures of boyhood exploring and sailing the waters of Choctawhatchee Bay along the North Florida Coast.

Attending school in those early days was a family affair, strictly on a do-it-yourself basis, with family chores not to be neglected. It was the times of a governess who "lived in" with the family and later the Little Red Schoolhouse several miles from home. You got there by walking or riding horseback, or else!

Mr. Reddick's growing up included the years of mischief and playing tricks, annual picnics, fishing and trapping animals, visiting nearby towns with streetcars, and listening to exciting Civil War stories told by his father as recalled later in a book titled *Seventy-Seven Years in Dixie*.

The spirit of adventure and self motivation is recorded in interesting detail beginning with the commercial boating that included timber, farm products, and alligator hides, then continuing on to a career in railroading when the stationmaster handled everything from passenger tickets to billing the freight. The steam locomotive was truly King of Travel in his early days, and the family excursion was a never-to-be-forgotten vacation thrill for family and friends.

Courtship and romance is told with humor and sincerity that led to Mr. Reddick's marriage to Miss Lillian Lea Anderson in Samson, Alabama. The following years relate interesting changes of assignment in his career with the railroad and the growth of his family that included daughters Lillian and Marion and a son, Homer.

Foreword

The excitement of a happy childhood, the pleasures of youth, and the fulfillment of a rewarding life with deep devotion to family, church, and fraternal friends are the dominant influences running through this interesting and marvelous recollection of life and times as written by Walker H. Reddick, Sr.

As I write these few words in appreciation for the good work and unfailing inspiration of Mr. Reddick, I am deeply mindful that I speak also for his wife and children, with whom I share grateful association.

– Carl Thomas Collins
Rome, Georgia
December 1977

PART I

Boyhood around the Choctawhatchee Bay

Chapter 1
So Many Brothers and Sisters

I was born in a small town in Washington County (now Walton County)—Point Washington, Florida, on May 5, 1889. There were two large sawmills in that town, and I would make a guess that the population was about two thousand. My father and mother each had previously been married and each had two small children. My mother had two boys, Will and Lafayette O'Neal; and my father had two girls, Ellen and Etta. And of their own children there were two girls and six boys—Jefferson, Tilden, Ida, Jeannette, Millard, John, Walker, and Guy—making a total of twelve children.

My father's name was Henry William Reddick and my mother's maiden name was Elizabeth G. McCormick, he being of Scottish descent and she of Scotch-Irish descent. My father had three brothers—James W., Madison, and George, and one sister, Sarah. All of them made their homes in and around Choctawhatchee Bay in western Florida.

After the end of the Civil War, my father purchased several thousand acres of timbered land on Four Mile Peninsula from the old Pensacola and Atlantic Railroad at twenty-five cents per acre. [The Louisville and Nashville Railroad gained control of the Pensacola and Atlantic Railroad in 1881.] The railroad had purchased the land for the cross-tie timber that was on it but later discovered that it would be too expensive to have the cross-ties cut and delivered to their nearest point of delivery, which was Pensacola. So they decided to sell the land to my father at this very nominal price.

My father operated two sawmills at this time, one on Garnier Bayou [now part of Ft. Walton Beach] and one at the head of Hogtown Bayou

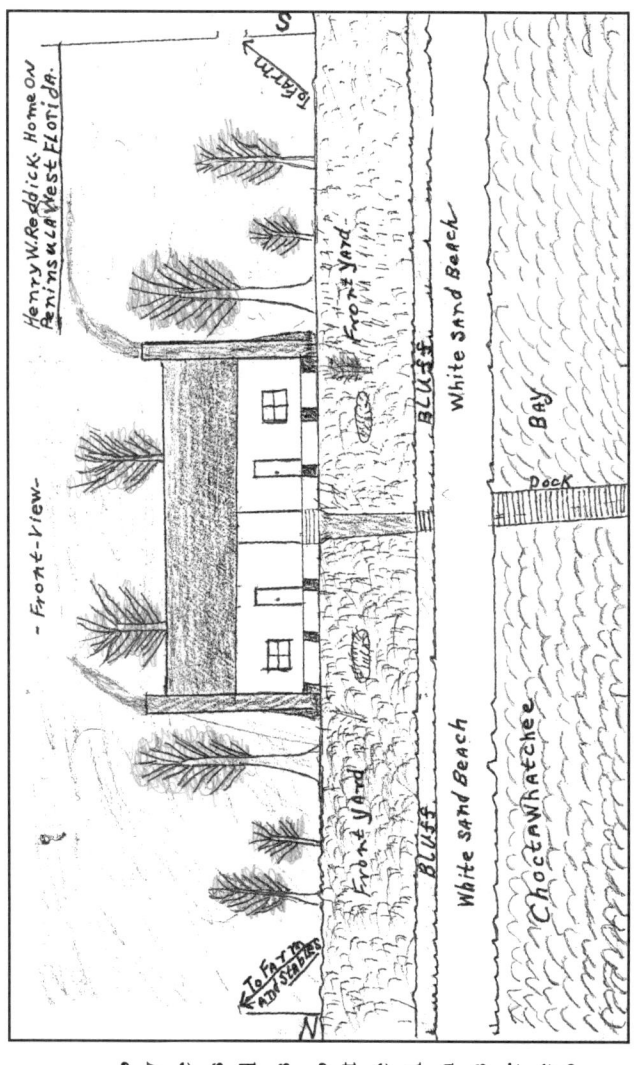

Front View
of the Reddick Home

"The house, when finished, was beautiful in every respect, with plenty of large rooms. This building was within about one hundred feet of the water's edge, this being Choctawhatchee Bay, and we could sit on our front porch and see almost to the western end of the Bay. A beautiful white sand beach added beauty to this magnificent home. The clear bottom of the Bay could be seen for a half mile." Drawing by the author.

on Choctawhatchee Bay. Father was passing by the William McCormick home on horseback one day and saw my mother standing in the yard. When he returned to his office at the mill he remarked to one of his employees that he saw a darn good-looking widow and he intended to make a date with her. He did and they became engaged and married shortly afterwards. He took his bride and built a home in Point Washington about fifteen miles from his mill.

When I was born, while my mother and father were living at Point Washington, a friend of my father was in town on business and noted that there was a new arrival in our home. He suggested that he name the newborn. His name was Walker Tervin of DeFuniak Springs, Florida, and he was in the livestock business. Mr. Tervin named me "Walker" and the "H" was added later. [The "H" doesn't stand for any name.] Mr. Tervin told my mother that when I was older he would send me a namesake gift. Four of my brothers and two sisters were also born at Point Washington and they attended school there. Also my mother's two boys by her first marriage and my father's two girls by his first marriage attended the Point Washington school.

My father decided that his family needed a larger house to live in as the family had grown so large. He conferred with my mother, and they decided that they would select a location on the land he had purchased from the railroad. Good timber was plentiful, and my father could cut the lumber in his sawmill up on Hogtown Bayou. The place they selected was about one mile south of Four Mile Point on the western shore of the peninsula. There was a very dense hammock with about fifty acres. The hammock was almost covered entirely with oyster shell mounds, and about ten inches under the topsoil there was a brown subsoil which was very adaptable for farming. We found after we moved there that we could grow most anything.

The lumber was cut and delivered. The house, when finished, was beautiful in every respect, with plenty of large rooms. This building was within about one hundred feet of the water's edge, this being Choctawhatchee Bay, and we could sit on our front porch and see almost to the western end of the Bay. A beautiful white sand beach added beauty to this magnificent home. The clear bottom of the Bay could be seen for a half mile. Also, we had a dock or pier that extended out about 150 feet from the shore, so the walk from the front porch reached all the way to the water. The yards were covered with Bermuda grass, and there were several large live oak trees which gave plenty of shade.

The house had five-foot-wide fireplaces, and we were always kept very comfortable, even in the cold winters. The dining room and kitchen were in a separate building about thirty feet from the main structure. While our dining room and kitchen were being finished, my mother had to cook on one of the large fireplaces. She had swinging pots and all kinds of ovens with top covers on them and fry pans. The ovens had three legs on them, and Mother would bake biscuits that were about four or five inches high and as white as snow. I remember eating five or six of them with good homemade syrup and butter. She also would cook vegetables in some kind of cookers. Mother did not have to cook on the fireplace long, though, because when the new kitchen was finished, it was furnished with a large range stove.

Mother and my two sisters were at-home packers of fresh meat and sausage-stuffers when hog-killing time came, which was when the weather turned cold, usually in December, and after we returned from our annual hunting expedition down at the Devil's Swamp on the peninsula. Mother made plenty of cottage cheese along with all the other dairy products. She also was in the poultry business raising chickens, ducks, turkeys, and guineas. Coops were made and all would be ready for shipment along with the other stock and oranges to our market in Pensacola.

Mother liked to cook cakes. John, Jeannette, and Ida would go out into the woods and pick huckleberries, blackberries, and blueberries, and she would add the berries to the muffins and cakes. She also was an expert on baking layer cakes.

Mother sometimes raked some oak ashes to one side of the fireplace and roasted some nice yam sweet potatoes. All of her food dishes were delicious and plentiful and served with plenty of milk and butter. All of us worked, and when we all sat down to that long table with a long bench on each side and a chair at each end, there was no telling how much food was consumed at each meal. My father took on the stray boys that came along (they did not have a home or mother or father), so the long benches on each side of the long table were always filled from end to end.

Let me tell you about the stray boys. In addition to their own family, my father and mother raised five white boys, their names were John Whittington, Hubert Worthen, Lee Barnes, Ernest Barnes, and Will Daniels, and two Negro boys, Henry Fowler and another by the name of Primas (given name—do not recall his surname). These boys did not come to our home at the same time, but as they came my father would take them in, clothe them, and send them to school (the school we attended on Four Mile Point). As soon as they were strong enough, Father would work them on the small farm near our home. My older brothers had a fishery over on the Gulf of Mexico, and when they (those taken in) did not have anything to do at home, he would send them over to work in the fishery.

I was quite young then, but later on in life I would occasionally meet some of them after they had left our home to make their own living. I was riding on the Louisville and Nashville train from Florala, Alabama, to Crestview, Florida, once, and when the conductor came through collecting tickets, he looked straight at me but passed on. I thought that face was familiar, and when he passed through again, he sat down on the seat beside me and asked me if I was one of the Reddick boys. I told him I was and he asked if I remembered him. I told him that his name was John Whittington. After the train stopped in Crestview he and I had a long talk.

On another occasion I met a man in Bainbridge, Georgia, at the newspaper stand one Sunday morning and recognized him as Will Daniels. He lived in New York and spent the winters in Bainbridge. Both men were surprised to see me.

I was in Freeport long after the two Negro boys were grown, and one of them put his hand on my shoulder and asked me if I remembered him. I told him to pull his hat off, he did, and I recognized the three birth marks on his head. I knew he was Henry Fowler. I never have seen Primas since he left us on Four Mile Point.

We had not lived in the new home very long before my mother and others of the family had cleared away grounds for all kinds of fruit trees including an orange grove. My father hired some men to help clear some land for a small farm, only about five acres to begin with. Later, as our cattle herd grew, we made pens to corral them so the land might be fertilized—we did not have commercial fertilizer in those days. And as time moved on we took in more of the hammock land, and in the end we had over twenty acres of farm land in cultivation. On our large range we had plenty of hogs which roamed almost beyond our land, and sometimes we would find some of them almost to the end of what is called now the Miracle Strip. [Highway 98 was designated as the Miracle Strip Parkway by the 1965 Legislature of Florida.] We raised feed for our stock and our four good milch cows for the winter and had four good horses to watch over all of them.

Chapter 2
Slow Horse Ride to School

I was about six years old at this time and my namesake, Walker Tervin, decided that I was old enough for him to fulfill his promise of that namesake gift. So one day a schooner [a fore-and-aft-rigged sailing vessel with at least two masts] anchored out in front of our home and there was my cow and calf. They threw the cow overboard and she swam ashore. They brought the calf ashore in a skiff [a flat-bottomed open boat of shallow draft, having a pointed bow and a square stern]. I immediately took charge of the calf. I saw that he was always fed well, and I often used a comb to keep him well groomed. He and his mother needed a name. My mother suggested that I call the cow Lon and the calf Dandy—the names suited me so that was their names.

As Dandy and I grew older I needed a wagon or cart and a yoke. My older brothers sawed off two wooden wheels from a large log and bored holes in the wheels for an axle. They finished the cart with shafts and body, also a bow and yoke—all of which put us into business.

My mother then gave me the job of hauling wood from the woods, which was plentiful and not too far off. When Mother and my two sisters did the laundry, they used a wash pot to heat the water, which used lots of wood. Also I had to keep enough wood for those large five-foot-wide fireplaces in the main building. The only pleasure I received out of all this was that I had a free ride to the woods and back. I think Dandy enjoyed it also.

It was not very long before I would be old enough to go to school, at which time I was seven-and-a-half years old. My older brothers and sisters were already in school except brother John. My father had engaged a cousin of ours for our governess and teacher.

Choctawhatchee Bay Around 1900

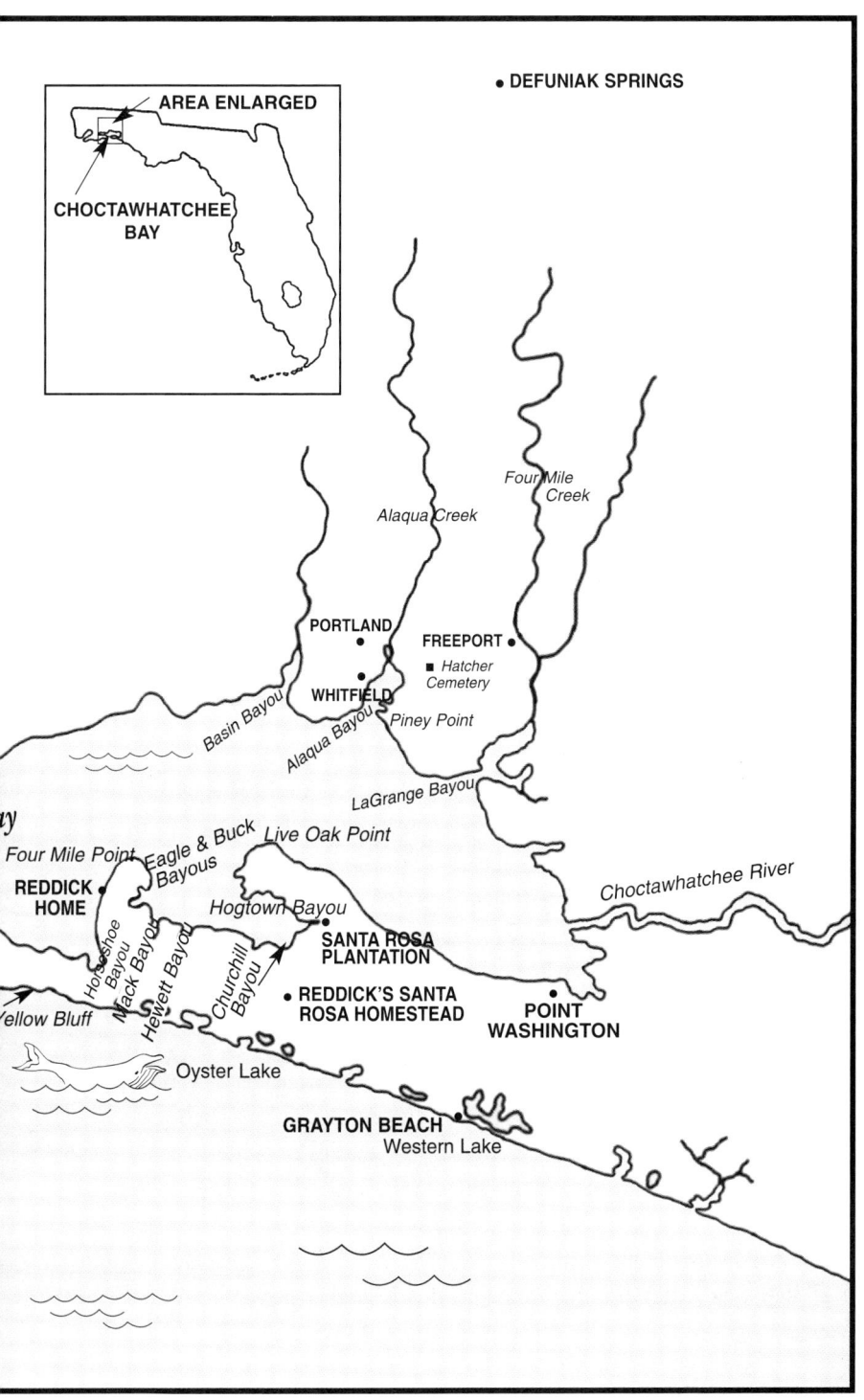

One of the large rooms in our home was used as a schoolroom. By this time another family, Bud Cook with wife and several small children of school age, had come across the Bay from a small village called Browntown. Living in the village were several families all related. Most of them were named Brown and some named Habbard and Cook.

Mr. Cook wanted a place to build a home, but my father would not sell him a piece of land but gave him permission to build any place he might select. So he looked around and decided on a large hammock covering about fifteen acres just south of our home. The hammock was of very rich soil, much like where our home was built. Mr. Cook built a small log house and a small barn and began clearing away some of the hammock to plant that year.

His children, four I think, came to our house to our private school. This school arrangement lasted one year, after which two other families moved in and built homes near us—they too had several children. The name of one of these families was Thomas. Mr. Thomas chose for his home site a top of a large sand dune on a piece of government land just up from the head of Horseshoe Bayou.

The other family, Mr. and Mrs. Hill, we did not know from whence they came, selected a building site on the east side of Horseshoe Bayou near the mouth. They only had one son named Lesco, and Mrs. Hill was a teacher.

There was a man named Thaggard that came in about this time who was a turpentine man and was leasing timbered land for turpentine business. After he had all the land leases he could get, including my father's, and after the trees were boxed and gum turpentine began to come in, Mr. Thaggard brought in lots of Negroes and some whites and built a large turpentine still about four or five miles east of our home.

With all of this increase in children population, my father decided that there would have to be education facilities provided for all these children as well as his. So he selected a spot about three-and-a-half miles from our home on the west side of Mack Bayou and about one hundred yards from a tributary which extended out from Buck Bayou. There was a nice boiling spring in this branch from which the school was furnished plenty of fresh pure and cool water.

I failed to mention that my father was on the school board at this time, and he built a nice school building and furnished it with all the equipment. Mrs. Hill was hired to teach. I was the youngest pupil in the school and five of us from our home had to ride an old gentle horse to school. I had to perch myself upon a tree stump and crawl on the one-horse caravan as it passed by—I had to ride behind and often slid off.

During school hours, being the youngest, I was allowed to go outside of the building and play. Some of the pupils, when they were excused to get a drink of water at the spring, would cut a reed and bow down over the spring and drink through the reed. I decided I would try my luck at this, so I found a reed that had been cut and left at the spring. I put it in my mouth and leaned myself over to get a drink. I became overbalanced and, with the reed in my mouth, plunged my head to the bottom of the spring. The reed ruptured a small blood vessel in my mouth, and I went screaming to the schoolhouse. The teacher thought that my injuries might be too serious to keep me in school so school was dismissed, and my brothers and sisters rode me home on the old gray horse. After examination by my mother, with a little sympathy, I was dismissed as a cured patient.

There was a small plot of land just east of the school building, which was selected as a burial plot in which my grandmother, Emily Skipper McCormick, was buried, as well as two older brothers and one younger brother. Several other people were buried there also. There was a road leading from the school building to the cemetery, which was located in the edge of the big hammock that covers all the land between the two bayous, Mack and Buck. There was also a road through the hammock that passed near the cemetery.

I mentioned about the Thomas family that built their home on the sand dune near Horseshoe Bayou. After the turpentine still had moved and the population of the area was on the increase, it was decided that there were enough patrons in the area to support a U. S. Post Office. My father and some others, through our congressman in Washington, D. C., were asked to do the necessary in getting a post office some place in the area.

It took some time but there was a post office authorized and Mr. Thomas was appointed postmaster. He had the office in his home and it was named Thomas, Florida. The mail was brought to the office by horse from Point Washington and the rider picked up the outgoing mail, returning to Point Washington.

We never did see Mr. Hill, the family that built their home on the east side of Horseshoe Bayou. He would come in and out to see his family, but as far as we knew no one ever met him. It developed some years after they had lived in their home that he had been apprehended in Louisiana and was charged with robbing trains in that area. The Hills planted a fig tree in their yard, and it grew and spread over several acres. Then the place was a hammock and it was called the Fig Hammock.

The Hills moved to New Orleans after Mrs. Hill taught in the new school. She and my mother were real good friends and carried on a lengthy correspondence after she moved. My mother gave me her last address after I had begun work with the Louisville and Nashville Railroad, and when I was in New Orleans once I visited Mrs. Hill. She was operating a candy and gift shop on Elizabeth Street. She informed me that her son Lesco had passed on, but she did not mention anything about her husband. I assumed that he also had passed on.

Chapter 3
First Train Ride

Vernon was the county seat of Washington County at this time. It was a small town in the northern section of the county. Superior Court was held there and my father most always received a summons by mail to serve on the jury. The distance from our home on Four Mile Point was about sixty-five miles, and the roads were bad to travel with horse and buggy, so my father had to ride one of the horses up there. Also there were some creeks to cross en route and after heavy rains the horse would have to swim.

Father would leave home early in the morning and ride to Pine Log, which was a crossing on Holmes Creek, then spend the night there with a friend and leave the next morning for the rest of the way. He would shell enough corn to feed the horse while up there and would divide the corn in a sack and carry it behind the saddle.

He knew many people in the county and liked politics enough that he would fight for his favorite candidate, especially when the political scene was the hottest. I remember he and General William Miller, at an election, had a fight. General Miller was in command of the Battle of Natural Bridge below Tallahassee, and his home after the Civil War was Point Washington. My father also had to pay his taxes while at the county seat. He most always took me with him, but it was too far for me to ride a horse to Vernon.

I remember my first train ride. Father had business in Chipley, Florida. I was about six years old and he thought I would like the ride. He said we would not be gone long so my mother prepared me with the necessary clothing (homemade suits), and we left home on a sailboat to Freeport. We caught a ride to DeFuniak Springs where we took the

General William Miller and the Point Washington School Children Circa 1890

Returning to Point Washington after the Civil War, General William Miller (in white sideburns) taught the local children in the "little red schoolhouse" built on a piece of Simeon Strickland's property. Miller, a veteran of the Mexican War (1846-1848), was forty years old and obtained the rank of major when he joined the Confederate Army. He led the First Florida Infantry Regiment in the Kentucky invasion and was later wounded at Murfreesboro, Tennessee. On August 2, 1864, he received the commission of brigadier general and was appointed commander of the reserve forces of Florida. General Miller served in the Florida House of Representatives in 1885 and the following year was elected to the State Senate. He died at his Point Washington home on August 8, 1909, at the age of eighty-nine. Courtesy, Albert Butler.

train about fifty miles to Chipley. This was the first train I ever saw. Father had many relatives in Chipley and we spent the night with one of them. On the way we would pass farm after farm of cotton; this was the first cotton I ever saw growing. All of this trip was a thrill to me, and after we had spent a few days there we returned home. I had plenty to tell my mother upon returning. Riding on the train was something new for me because I had never ridden anything except a boat or horse pulling a wagon or a yoke of oxen pulling a cart.

When I reached the age of about seven, my father bought me a rifle in the caliber of twenty-two short. It could be used as a rifle or as a pistol. The stock was made of an iron rod twisted so as to form the shape of a stock, and you could push the stock into a groove outside of the barrel to make a pistol grip. I was afraid of the thing, but I was taught how to use it and always cautioned about the danger of it.

My daddy wanted to make me a man as soon as he could—since I was the baby—as he needed someone to go with him when he would go hunting. One day he told my mother that he was taking me hunting with him. He saddled two of the horses and we started out. As we approached one of the lakes near the Gulf about four miles from home, the dogs struck a trail. This lake is near what is known now as Four Mile Village.

As the dogs were running something around the lake, we stopped the horses ahead of the dogs and waited. As the dogs drew near we saw a bobcat climbing a dead pine tree—the tree was surrounded by a patch of palmetto. The cat climbed up to a fork in the tree and faced the dogs. My daddy told me to take his large ten-gauge gun and go down near the tree and shoot the cat. I did so reluctantly and half scared to death. By the time I reached a point close to the tree, I cocked both barrels, and, as I raised the gun to shoot, the cat reversed his position, facing me, and leaped out towards me. I did not have time to shoot as he was practically on me. My daddy was watching me all the time. I ran out where he was holding the horses, dragging the gun, as it was too heavy for me to carry any other way. He had a good joke on me and liked to tell about it when we arrived home. The bobcat got away unharmed.

Later as I grew older I was allowed to have a shotgun, but before

I had a shotgun of my own, I was out on the dock in front of our home, and I saw a duck swimming towards the beach. I ran to the house and put two shells in my daddy's ten-gauge gun and eased down behind some shrubbery, and when I saw the duck I was almost close enough to put the barrel of the gun on him. I cocked both barrels and let him have it. The gun kicked me over on my back, and after the smoke cleared away I went into the water and brought in my kill. He was almost shot to pieces. I took him to the house and my mother cooked him—you can imagine how large I felt. I went on many hunts with my father after that experience.

My father worked hard and expected all of the rest to do the same. By the time I was seven years old I had to do certain chores, and brother John, two years older than I, was assigned tougher and much harder work. Of course, this work was carried on at home in between schools. After we had worked all the week up to Saturday noon we were allowed to do anything we cared to do.

Both of us preferred fishing, sometimes on the Bay side of the peninsula for saltwater fish, and then sometimes we would fish in Buck Bayou or Eagle Bayou. Sometimes we would pull the skiff around to Mack Bayou where we could catch trout and bream with hook and line. We had to dig in the earth for worms to use as fish bait for the fresh water fishing, and sometimes we would find a catawba tree with hundreds of worms.

If we did not prefer fishing on our half day off from our work, we would make traps and catch birds. The traps were made of thin slats stacked on top of each other to build a pyramid-shaped house using long slats on the sides and short slats on each end. To hold the slats together, we used one slat across the top crosswise and would bind the slat by tying one down to the bottom slat on one end and doing the same on the other end. Then we would prop one end of the trap up with a stick perpendicular with a notched treadle, extending the stick out in front of the trap which fit into another stick that was placed on top of the perpendicular stick. The treadle extended back into the trap with the end an inch or two off the ground. Grain was placed under the treadle, and when the birds began eating, they would touch the treadle and the trap would fall.

I remember brother John and I caught a trap full of quail. As he would reach under the trap and pull out a bird, I would take the bird and tie both legs with a string and lay them on the ground. After John had them all out, which must have been at least a dozen or more, all the birds flew off. We were certainly two surprised boys.

There were many other ways we could use our half day off, but this seemed to be our favorite. We had a flock of wild goats roaming the woods, and sometimes we would get out into the woods and try to catch one. But most of the time the goats could run much faster than we. The two Negro boys also had the Saturday afternoon off and would enjoy fishing and chasing goats with John and me.

Brother John and I, at our age at that time, wanted to make some money of our own, so we decided to do some fishing, and the fish we caught could be easily disposed of at fancy prices (five cents per fish). We made some sharp spears and caught flounders as they came near to the edge of the beach and covered themselves with sand. They did this so the small fish wouldn't see them and a flounder would snap and catch his food. We took a sack along, each of us did, and John would go one direction and I would go the other. As we speared a flounder, we would leave him on the white sand beach, and when we thought we had about as many as we could carry, we would start walking back picking up our fish, and most always we would have both sacks full. Then we would take a horse and wagon and haul our catch over to Mr. Thaggard's turpentine still and peddle those fish out in just a short while and return home with two Bull Durham tobacco sacks full of nickels and dimes.

Chapter 4
Sailing to Pensacola

We saved our money until my father had decided to take a load of cattle and hogs to market in Pensacola. My mother always had several coops of chickens, turkeys, and ducks. Also we would take some wild goats along. Pens were made on the deck of the schooner for the livestock, and the rest of the cargo was put in the hold of the boat. If this trip to market was scheduled for late fall or winter, we would give an orange picking contest and take along, with the other items mentioned, fifty or sixty crates of oranges, putting them below deck. We had no trouble disposing of the cargo—everything that we had on the boat was already sold to a chain meat market operator whose last name was Nealy. We always unloaded at Palafox Street wharf, and Mr. Nealy had teams there to haul our cargo off to his markets.

Brother John and I would always have enough money saved from our fish sales to buy all our school supplies and most of our clothing while we were on one of our trips to Pensacola. I remember on one of our trips, after our cargo had been unloaded, my mother would take one of us down in the cabin of the boat to give us a bath and put on our new home-made clothes. I will never forget how hard she could rub with a wet cloth behind my ears, but I suppose I needed it.

After she had finished with me, all dressed up in my home-made waist and pants, she sent me out on deck to wait until she had finished with brother John. There was a fifty-gallon water barrel on deck next to the cabin, with a square hole in the top so the water could be gotten out when needed, and the flap that covered the hole was put on with tacks. To keep myself clean on the deck and wait for her to get through with brother John, I sat down on the water barrel and over the tacked-on flap that covered the hole.

When all were bathed and dressed to go uptown to do our shopping, I jumped off of the barrel, and some of those tacks had worked through my nice home-made pants and tore almost all of the seat out. When my mother discovered this, she took me down across her lap and spanked me about all I could stand, then she took needle and thread and tried to get as much of the damage together as she could. We then started up Palafox Street and I had to walk sidewise to hide the part that my mother did not see when sewing me up. But we made it up to one of the large stores and purchased our supplies and returned to the boat.

On another trip to Pensacola, with another cargo of about the same as we had on the trip before, John and I were large enough to wash our own necks and don our tailor-made-at-home clothes, and we were allowed to go uptown without an escort. There were no amusements much or any kind of devilment that we could get into, but we took in the town and went to the old three-story vaudeville theater that was on Gadsden Street, as I remember. Besides the show that was on, we had plenty of peanuts, and as we were always in the peanut gallery we could throw out hulls down on the heads of the audience below.

There were streetcars on Palafox Street—the cars ran on wooden rails and were drawn by two large horses. You could step on and step off at any place whether the car was stopped or moving.

My father had many friends in Pensacola that he sometimes visited, and on one occasion I remember that we were visiting one of his friends named Mr. Crowberger. He had a son named Jimmy. Mr. Crowberger was the chief of police and had an office in the police station where there were several policemen sitting around waiting to go on duty. Jimmy took John and me to the police station one night, and the police thought they would have some fun so they took after us and caught us down on another street. They told us that we were arrested for loitering and that we would be locked up. We thought that it was no joke but they locked us up in one of the police wagons that was nearby and kept us in there almost all night. I have never liked policemen ever since this happened.

Pensacola Wharf—Circa 1910

Pensacola boasted a population of over thirteen thousand at the turn of the twentieth century. The families scattered along Choctawhatchee Bay and its rivers took two or three days to sail to Pensacola to bring their chickens, turkeys, cattle, and home-grown produce to market. Their schooners lined the wharf at the end of Palafox Street—one of sixteen wharves in Pensacola—to unload their cargoes and reload with provisions of sugar, flour, and coffee. Courtesy, Florida State Archives.

Boyhood around the Choctawhatchee Bay

Brother John and I had other ways of making our money by trapping small animals, such as opossums, raccoons, otters, and foxes. We would set our traps around the edges of ponds and about the edges of the two bayous about two miles east of our home, Buck and Eagle Bayous. We would visit the traps once a day and sometimes we would have seven or eight such animals. Then we would skin them and stretch their hides on boards to dry out.

Another way we had of making money was killing alligators in some of the ponds and in the bayous. We had a coal miner's light, which was buckled about the head, and we could see the eyes of an alligator two hundred yards away. I very quietly sculled the boat to the alligator, and John would shoot him with a thirty-thirty Winchester rifle. An alligator sank quickly, but I always had a pole with a large hook on one end of it that I would get around him. Then both of us would get around him and pull him along beside the boat and haul him in. This operation had to be done immediately after the kill or we would lose him. We hunted in Horseshoe Bayou many times and killed some as long as twelve feet.

When we had killed all we could in the bayous, we would haul our skiff over to the lakes near the Gulf where we would find some huge ones, as there was no alligator hunting in those lakes that we knew of. We would kill most all night, and when daylight came we would pull them ashore and skin them and salt the hides away to keep them from spoiling. When we had a lot of the small animal skins and alligator hides, we would pack them in boxes and ship them to St. Louis. They would pay us about twenty-five cents apiece for the small animal skins and twenty-five cents per foot for the alligator skins. But we thought we were cheated because sometimes the fur company would reduce the price on account, they would say, that the skins were not of the best quality.

The railroad that had sold Father the timbered land on Four Mile Point was badly in need of cross-ties. They sent their agent, Mr. George Rushbridge, to our home to talk with my father about cutting ties from the land which they had almost given away and shipping them to Pensacola. The proposition put to my father was that the railroad would accept the cross-ties F.O.B. loaded on barges the railroad would send to Buck Bayou, and when several were loaded they would have a steamboat tow them to Pensacola.

My father accepted their proposition (I do not remember the price involved) and employed several crews to cut the ties and haul them to the loading landing on the west side of Buck Bayou. The reason Buck Bayou was chosen was because the entrance to Mack Bayou was too shallow to get the barges out after they were loaded, and Buck Bayou had a deeper channel at that time. My pet calf Dandy had grown to be large enough to work instead of play, so my father had him put in one of the working teams hauling cross-ties.

The business of cutting the timber and hewing out the ties and hauling them to the landing went on for several weeks. As soon as Father thought that they had several barge loads, he would send for the barges, and they would load all of them. When four or five were loaded, the railroad would send a steamboat to tow them to Pensacola. This operation continued until the railroad advised that they would not need more ties for some time.

Mr. Rushbridge continued to come up to our home on Four Mile Point and would bring a party with him sometimes, and my father would take them deer hunting. I remember one time they brought a fine ten-gauge double-barreled shotgun with them which was to be given to the man that killed the most deer. My father killed the most—I think he killed four—and the Parker gun was given to him. The friendship between my father and Mr. Rushbridge grew stronger and they often visited each other.

There was a wide hallway through the middle of our home and I remember seeing seven large buck deer hanging at one time in that hall. After the deer were dressed their horns would be attached to the walls of that hall and were used as coat and hat racks. My father often picked up young fawns on his hunts and brought them home. My mother would raise them until they were almost grown and then turn them loose to be wild again for the sportsmen to find and kill.

A man representing a hunting club in Birmingham, Alabama, came to our home one day in the summer looking for a place to make a camp for the club members to live when they arrived on the Bay in the winter. My father took the man over on Eagle Bayou which was about two miles from our home.

Boyhood around the Choctawhatchee Bay

There was a small peninsula between the Bay line from Four Mile Point and Eagle Bayou which contained about five acres with lots of live oaks with swinging moss—a beautiful spot for a house such as the man wanted for the club. The Bay on one side and the bayou on the other would make a good harbor for any boats they may have. The man bought the five acres from my father and a deed was made. The man wanted a house built on the land and he selected a spot on the bayou side in between two large oak trees. Next, the problem of getting someone to build the house arose.

My father told him that his two small sons were very good carpenters, and with his supervision, he thought he could get the house built by the time the hunting club would want to come down for their duck hunt in the winter. This satisfied the man.

Brother John and I were just boys then, but we would not turn down that job of building the house. The material was all figured out, nails, roofing, etc. There was a small sawmill at the head of Hogtown Bayou, now Santa Rosa, that we could bring lumber down to by boat. We could buy the nails and other supplies in Freeport.

We borrowed my father's large sloop [a single-masted, fore-and-aft-rigged sailing boat] and sailed up to the sawmill and bought a load of lumber, loading it crosswise on the deck, which made the boat top-heavy. We set sail for Eagle Bayou, and a storm came up when we were off Hewett Bayou. The boat capsized and all the lumber drifted ashore. We stayed with the boat until the storm was over, at which time she had drifted into shallow water. We lowered the sails and tied them to the booms. We pumped all the water out using the hand pump and managed to upright the boat. Then we poled the boat into Hewett Bayou and anchored her.

We proceeded to pick up the lumber that had drifted ashore, and we did get the most of it. We reloaded it on the boat and sailed on to Eagle Bayou, unloading it where the house was to be built. Then we sailed to Freeport and bought the rest of the supplies and started to work. We finished the house and my father mailed the club the bill and they mailed him the check. Father paid John and me what I think was about two hundred dollars for our work. In fact it was more money than we had ever seen before.

Chapter 5
Fun and Frolic at Oyster Lake

It was school time again for brother John and me, so both of us were boarded out with our two half sisters at Point Washington. I stayed with sister Etta McDonald and brother John with sister Ellen Grace. Etta had six children and Ellen had six, so you can see that when John and I crowded in with them, there were two big families.

This was a four-month school, and we hardly got started before school was out for that year. We were most always in the same grade because we studied the same books every year—we never knew when we would be advanced to a higher set of books. This was typical of all the schools in the area. But when we studied the same books for three or four years we were well prepared educationally for promotion to the next set of books (grade).

This situation could not be the fault of the school board because they were doing their best to improve the schools. Most of the teachers were high school students—very few had a college education. Our school building was a two-story frame structure and always crowded. Wooden desks and chairs for double seating did not give us room to be comfortable.

It was about a mile from where sister Etta lived to the school, and we had to walk a narrow path through thick shrubbery and blackjack trees. There was a creek with a footlog across it that all the rest could run across without falling off, but I most always slipped into the water and my clothes were wet most of the day. We had some pot-bellied stoves that would dry out our clothes. Our games were baseball, bullpen, and softball. Some of the courting crowd would sit out under the shade of the large pine trees and talk.

The back of one of the large rooms had a platform which was made for Friday afternoon speeches, and most everyone in my room had to recite, and, as I remember, about once a month all the school board would visit the school. My father was on the board and I was supposed to do extra well when he was there, or I would have to explain why I did not—I most always got by, though.

My mother was a devout Christian in every respect—she did not only practice her religion but she lived it. There were no churches in the vicinity of our home, none closer than Point Washington which was about twenty miles from our home. Brother John and I were taught to observe the Sabbath Day and were not allowed to carry on any kind of activity. If we were at home from school or were staying at home between schools, we had to observe the Sabbath and keep it holy.

Each Sunday morning, after we had finished breakfast and the dishes were washed and the cows attended to, Mother would have John and me gather beside her in one of the rooms in the large house, she with the Bible on her lap and both of us kneeling so we could have our eyes on the Bible while she read the scriptures to us. After she had read one or two chapters she would try to explain what wrath would be upon us if we did not obey God, which amounted to a well prepared sermon.

While we were in school at Point Washington, Mother would visit us about once a month or as often as she could. It was about twenty miles from our home on Four Mile Point to Point Washington and she would drive one of the horses up there, usually on Saturday, over very bad roads, and take John and me to the Baptist Church—the church she belonged to. She would start back to our home on Four Mile Point on Monday morning, taking all day for the trip. The roads that she had to travel over were part mud and part deep sand with plenty of large pine tree roots to make it really bumpy. The times that she did not get to visit us we would attend the Methodist Church Sunday school and church services. This church was closer and not so far to walk.

We always had plenty of work to do but often took time off to have fun and frolic. Once a year we would get all of the family together, including all the young boys that took up at our home, including the two Negro boys, and grease all the wagons, buggies, and cart axles and

Mother, Elizabeth G. Reddick

"Each Sunday morning, after we had finished breakfast and the dishes were washed and the cows attended to, Mother would have John and me gather beside her in one of the rooms in the large house, she with the Bible on her lap and both of us kneeling so we could have our eyes on the Bible while she read the scriptures to us." Courtesy, Florida State Archives.

make all preparations for a two-days' outing. All of these vehicles were drawn by horses and oxen over the roughest roads in the country. Our destination was Oyster Lake, one of the most beautiful lakes near the Gulf located about fifteen miles east from our home on Four Mile Point.

It took most of the first day to make the trip because we were not able to make the speed limit, much less break it. We had a camp site already selected before we arrived. It was down beside the lake and between two tall sand dunes. We spread an awning over the top of the scrub trees and scattered blankets and quilts on the sand, making a very nice cushioned floor.

My mother and both of my sisters, Ida and Jeannette, always saw that we had plenty of food, such as cakes and potato pies and some other good eats. Besides, we had plenty of strong coffee brewed at the camp. This food was well packed in two or three turtleback trunks.

If the water was very high in the lake, the men would dig a trench from the lake to the Gulf just deep enough to get the water started to run. This action of ours would soon lower the water in the lake enough for us to catch the fish before they followed the water into the Gulf. And the water being low in the lake made it easy to gather the oysters. You can see what fun we had.

There was no one living near the lake at that time, but this being government land, an old gentleman and his son by the name of Sowell built them a small hut on a hill overlooking the lake. They caught rattlesnakes and shipped their skins north, and, of course, they practically lived off of the fish and oysters. The old gentleman soon died and the son took unto himself a wife, a widow by the name of Mrs. White. He claimed the rights to the lake and its contents, so that ended our frolic and fun each year. But another gala picnic and boat excursion took us to Santa Rosa Island.

During my boyhood days, July Fourth was a very special day in and around all of the small towns on Choctawhatchee Bay. It was widely known that this very special day would be celebrated in the usual way, that is, without written invitation, as all were geared for a two-day picnic and dance on Santa Rosa Island.

Many of the sawmills shipped most of their lumber by large barges

Oyster Lake—Circa 1940

One can see the beauty of Oyster Lake where the Reddick family traveled for fun and frolic forty years earlier. Courtesy Jeanne Allen Newsom.

towed by the steamer *Florida*, a large stern-wheel tow steamer. The barges were loaded with lumber at the various sawmills on the Bay and the *Florida* would pick them up, four or five each tow, and take them to Pensacola. I have mentioned about the barges and the steamer to give you an idea about how much interest was shown in this special celebration, July Fourth, by doing it the elaborate way.

Of course, each family that participated in this two-day picnic and dance took ample food, such as pies and cakes. Sometimes a barbecued pig would be in one of the food chests that was brought along, and it would be put on one of the large tables on the barge. The pig would have in his mouth an apple and red-white-and-blue ribbons about his neck, which made his appearance very colorful. Food was plentiful—no one went away hungry.

As the caravan of barges was towed down the Bay by the steamer, other smaller boats would be out in the Bay waiting to tie onto the three-barge caravan, making the tow have the appearance of a locomotive pulling a long train. Platforms were erected on the barges for dancing, and there was always plenty of good musicians along—fiddlers. Blackberry wine was plentiful in jugs that had corncob stoppers sealed with cooked resin. Some of the wine had been put up and stowed away in a barn for several years.

The destination for the landing of the barges was on the Narrows at a point almost opposite of Mary Esther on Santa Rosa Island. The spot was well known as the "Ladies Walk," so named because of the absence of sand dunes. The sand was as white as snow and without a spot or wrinkle. There was some grief and sorrow when time came to make our way back to our homes knowing that it would be another year before this time would be with us again. We would have to be seriously ill not to partake in the next celebration.

Chapter 6
Hog Hunting near Devil's Swamp

The buildings at our home on Four Mile Point—consisting of the main house, separate kitchen and dining room, a large storeroom, a small room that we called the saddle room, a smokehouse, a large barn and stables for the horses, and a tool room—more often needed repair, especially the roofs. There was no such thing as composition roofing then so we had to make our own roofing.

Occasionally a large cypress log would drift ashore, coming down from Choctawhatchee River and washing high up on the beach. When one of the buildings needed a roof, we would saw one of these cypress logs into the desired blocks and then split the blocks into four or six pieces. Using a froe, a long blade with an upright handle in one end of it, we would rive the blocks into boards as thick or as thin as we desired. We would buy small nails at the store, then we'd cover the building with the boards. Cypress boards seldom ever rot or leak when put on properly. One large cypress log would re-cover several buildings.

Lumber needed for fences was not much of a problem, as we could cut pine timber from our land and tow it across the Bay to a sawmill and have it sawed into lumber. It sounds like lots of trouble to get this kind of materials, but at the time it was the only way.

When a plow stock was needed, my father would make one out of seasoned hickory with all the parts. I have plowed with one of these homemade plow stocks year after year before a new one would have to be made. My father would make a pen out of lightwood logs [anything but lightweight, lightwood logs were the heart of dead pines, used by the pioneers as a source of light] and fill it with oyster shells and burn them into lime. Lime was often needed in repairing chimneys. There were oyster shell mounds all about the place, placed there by the Indians, and as we would dig into them we would often find clay pots, arrowheads, and other things the Indians used.

There was very little that we had to buy—we were almost self-supported. My father always had to have his cornbread so we had a hand gristmill that made good meal. We grew vegetables most all the year around and my mother canned all the fruits and vegetables to last through the winter. All kinds of berries were growing about the home place and in the woods. To get meat, most any kind we wanted, all we had to do was go out into the woods.

After the crops had been gathered and stowed away in the barns and all the pumpkins and kershaws were mixed in with the corn in the crib (because they were planted in the same field with the corn) and were stored in a dry place so they would keep through the winter, then it was cane-grinding time. We only made three barrels of syrup, which was more than we could use, but the Negroes at the turpentine still about four miles east of us would come to our home often to buy syrup, milk, and vegetables.

Winter was about to make its appearance and the next thing in order was hog killing. We usually kept two or three hogs in pens at home for immediate use when our meat supplies began to run low. But the main killing and butchering was when the men all got together and planned our regular hunt down on the peninsula near Destin.

Some rode horses, some traveled in wagons, and some sailed down and landed at the head of Jones Bayou. The crowd that rode down hunted along the way, and when we all met at our camp on Jones Bayou, they most always had killed a deer or two. We pitched a tent for cover on the banks of the bayou and others batched on the boat. The Devil's Swamp was near the camp.

I was a small boy at that time and my weapon was a twenty-two caliber rifle. The men would leave me at the camp to take care of everything, but I stayed on the boat most of the time. There was a hog trail leading down into the swamp, partly obscured by tall grass and shrubbery. One day I was reconnoitering about the camp and I saw the grass and shrubbery moving about. The hair on my head began to rise.

Back View
of the Reddick Home

"The buildings at our home on Four Mile Point—consisting of the main house, separate kitchen and dining room, a large storeroom, a small room that we called the saddle room, a smokehouse, a large barn and stables for the horses, and a tool room—more often needed repair, especially the roofs." Drawing by the author.

I thought it could be a bear—there had been some seen one time in the swamp. I was not going to risk the rifle I had for protection, so I immediately jumped aboard the boat and peeped out the window and saw what my imagination was. It was a large hog that the dogs had chased out of the swamp, and when he saw me he ran the other way.

When the hunters came back to the camp late in the evening they'd have some hogs that had to be dressed and salted away in the barrels that we had for that purpose. Also a deer would have to be skinned and dressed and salted away. Sometimes they would bring in a wild turkey or two. We'd cook the turkeys. When the hunt was over, after we had been down there for almost two weeks, we'd head back home with all the meat we wanted and some for the neighbors.

There were two foreigners that lived near our hunting territory on the Peninsula near Destin—Mr. Haugen and Mr. A. P. Bjorklund, from Sweden. They came to this country together and homesteaded on adjoining homesteads. [The Homestead Act was passed by Congress in 1862 promising ownership of a 160-acre tract of public land to a citizen who had resided on and cultivated the land for five years after the initial claim.]

Mr. Bjorklund was a newspaper man. He did not live on his place very long because he did not know how to farm, that not being his occupation. So he abandoned his place and moved to Freeport on the other side of the Bay and established a weekly newspaper, the *Freeport Observer*.

Mr. Haugen's home was near the beach, and, being a good ship carpenter and builder, he soon started to build one of the nicest and the first liquid-fuel boat on Choctawhatchee Bay, her name, the *Mayflower*. The liquid fuel was called naphtha oil, some kind of refined kerosene, I think. This nice boat had an upright engine in it, and all you had to do to start the engine was to light a match and drop it through a small opening into the engine, and it would begin popping.

Some company in Freeport bought the boat and put it into mail and passenger service between Freeport and Point Washington, and it was mastered by Mr. Eugene Rutan. You could hear it popping for about two miles. If you were going to meet the boat at Point Washington to greet someone coming in, you would not have to watch for the time for

The Steamboat *Captain Fritz* on Choctawhatchee Bay
Circa early 1900s

The *Captain Fritz* was operated on the Holmes Creek/ Choctawhatchee River-to-Pensacola run from 1892 to 1936, hauling freight and carrying passengers to the small towns along Choctawhatchee Bay. "It was only about four miles across the Bay to White Point, and on fair days we could see all the boats going and coming from a view on our porch."

Boyhood around the Choctawhatchee Bay

the boat to land because you could hear the popping some time before its arrival. Meeting the boat reminded me of the crowds in small towns meeting the trains—you could always tell about the size of the town by the size of the crowd at the depot when the train was to arrive.

The Point Washington post office was just up on the hill from the boat landing, and after the mail was delivered to the post office, several of us kids, I mean devilish boys, would scuffle in the lobby of the office and Mr. Mundy, an old gentleman, would scold us. Sometimes he would come out and run us out, but we would come back and worry him some more. Some of the boys would call him "old man Mundy on Friday" or whatever day it happened to be. It would make him mad, and at times he would lock the door so we could not get back into the lobby to tease him.

I remember the Pattens that lived in Point Washington, and they had some relatives that lived in Long Island, New York. I do not remember the names of the relatives, but I do remember that they came to visit the Pattens. There was a pretty little girl in the family that I became very much attached to. We corresponded for some time after she returned to Long Island. Their visits were quite often, and I would meet the mail boat when I knew they were coming.

It was only about four miles across the Bay to White Point, and on fair days we could see all the boats going and coming from a view on our porch. The old steamer *Florida*, towing about four or five barges of lumber from up the Choctawhatchee Bay, would pass about twice a week, and sailboats of many sizes would be sailing towards Pensacola with their cargoes. Then the old *Captain Fritz* with her cargo of many kinds of freight and passengers would pass about two times each week. I made a few trips to Pensacola on the *Captain Fritz* as a passenger, I think the round trip fare was six dollars which included meals and room. If you have never traveled by water on one of these passenger steamers you will never know what an appetite you can have. Captain John Rogers on the *Captain Fritz* was always so nice and attentive to his passengers and would do all he possibly could to make the trip enjoyable.

Other steamboats I remember on the Bay were the *Ruth* and the *Dewey*. These were smaller boats and they would go up the river and bring out naval stores and take them to market in Pensacola. I think the *Ruth* sank with a cargo of resin on the Santa Rosa Sound across from the quarantine station below Pensacola.

Chapter 7
Whale of a Tale

There was a family who moved from Saskatchewan, Canada, and homesteaded a piece of land about six miles east of our home. Their names were Mr. and Mrs. Matthews and two daughters, Pearl and Ruby. They moved in a covered wagon drawn by two of the largest mules I ever saw. They were fine people, and the girls were about the ages of brother John and me.

On Sunday afternoons John and I rode two of the horses up to see the girls. The girls would ride the two mules, and we would all ride over to the Gulf, which was only about a mile from where the Matthewses lived. We would stroll on the Gulf beach and pick up shells and coconuts that washed ashore.

Mr. Matthews told us that when they left Canada they did not have the least idea where they would locate in western Florida, but they kept driving and came to the spot where he filed on the piece of land. They lived in the covered wagon until he built a house and afterwards he cleared part of the land and began to grow a small farm.

Mrs. Matthews could make the best light bread that I ever ate, also fudge candy. Besides making the trips to see the girls, we were lured in that direction to partake of some of the good bread and fudge.

I heard from Ruby after I left our home on Four Mile Point. I have a postcard in my possession at this time which was postmarked at Santa Rosa, Florida, dated December 23, 1911, from Miss Ruby Matthews. She was attending school in Santa Rosa at the time.

The atmosphere on the peninsula was much warmer than it was on the mainland, the north side of the Bay. This was due to the wind currents from the mainland and Bay meeting the Gulf currents, causing

Old Freeport Waterfront—Circa 1890

Warehouses line the wharf, with turpentine barrels out front ready to be taken to Pensacola. The mail launch (flying the U. S. flag) has arrived, a sailing schooner is tied up on the south shore, and with smoke boiling from her smokestack, a steamboat is coming up the channel. Courtesy, J. Lamar and Wanda Ward, Freeport Archival Collection.

a warmer climate. This made it more adaptable for growing an early vegetable crop.

My father always had ripe watermelons on the market one month before they had them on the north side of the Bay, all of which demanded a better price. Our market for the melons was Freeport. When the melons were ripe, and my father could always tell by placing an age mark on them, we would pull them from the vines, haul them to the water to load them on a skiff, then transfer them to the large sloop anchored farther out in deeper water. After we had the boat loaded and had enough wind, we would take off for Freeport, which was four miles up a deep creek from LaGrange Bayou. After we sailed out of the bayou and entered the creek, the tall timber on either side deleted the wind and most of the time we had to pole up the creek. One of us had to use a pole to put against the land and push the boat while the other one had to steer the boat close to land.

There were several stores in Freeport and all of them were always anxious to buy our melons. After we unloaded the boat and the shopping was done (we did not have to shop for anything except sugar, coffee, rice, and meal), my father always had to get his Bull Durham and Dukes mixture smoking tobacco, as he smoked a pipe. This was where I got into trouble.

Like many other boys of my age, I thought I should do as my father did. I always had a few melons of my own that I raised myself and could use the money as I pleased. On one of our trips to Freeport I decided that I would buy my own tobacco and quit stealing his. So when the store delivered the groceries down to the boat in a box, my two or three sacks of Bull Durham tobacco and cigarette papers were in a separate paper sack from his.

After we had sailed out onto the Bay my father always had me steer the boat while he went down into the cabin and checked on the groceries. When he came back on deck he said to me, "Walker, they made a mistake in filling my order for tobacco. They gave me two sacks with tobacco in each one of them." I had to keep my mouth shut and continue stealing his tobacco until he caught up with me later on. I confessed when I was almost grown. He said he had always wondered about that tobacco.

My father's birthday was June 16, and this date was always remembered in the Choctawhatchee Bay area as everybody was invited to celebrate with him on this occasion. My mother and two sisters, Jeannette and Ida, began making plans about one month before this date, getting everything together as far as the food was concerned. It took about three weeks to prepare the food for the over one hundred guests that would attend the party.

The men of the family began getting material on the ground for erecting the eighty-foot table and extra benches for the crowd that was anticipated to attend this birthday party. Most of the benches and table materials were stored under a shed to be used each year.

The long table was erected on the beautiful Bermuda grass lawn in the front yard. It was a sight to see all the food of most anyone's taste and the three barbecued whole pigs—one at each end of the table and one in the middle. Each pig was decorated with a red, white, and blue ribbon about its neck and each had a red apple in its mouth. The large living room (parlor) and another large room were cleared of all furniture for all that wanted to dance.

On the morning of June the sixteenth, there were anchored in front of our home thirty-five or more boats, and skiff-load after skiff-load landed the crowd. Some from DeFuniak Springs, Freeport, Niceville (then Boggy Bayou), Whitfield, Destin, and some from Pensacola. My father entertained those who wanted to look around the beautiful yard and the farms, especially his watermelon patches. They would pull enough melons to serve all who wanted to eat them. Usually around ten o'clock a nice swift and refreshing breeze from the shore kept everybody cool. Some that brought their bathing suits would enjoy bathing in the clear-bottomed Bay.

There were always two or three fiddlers in the crowd to furnish music for the dancing. Dancing would begin after the noon meal and would continue until daylight the next morning when the party would break up, and all would gather around my father and wish him many more happy birthdays. The party was over until the next year when we would go through the same thing.

On one of our Saturday afternoons off, brother John and I decided to ride over to one of the lakes near the Gulf and just across from the

Horseshoe Bayou. All the horses had been working all the week and were resting for the next week, so the only one that we could get to ride was a mustang [a small, hardy wild horse, brought to the New World by Spanish explorers]. She was very tricky and afraid of everything. Our object was to catch one of the large soft-shell turtles and take some turtle eggs home.

We used an iron rod to locate the turtle nests and eggs. The turtles would scratch out a round hole about six or seven inches deep and lay their eggs in it. We would push the rod into the ground near where the turtles came out to lay, and when we found a soft spot in the ground and the rod would pierce the eggs, we'd scratch the eggs out and put them in a sack.

On this trip we knew that the mustang would not let us take the turtle on her back with us, so we tied her to a tree before we arrived at the lake and walked on. We found and caught one of the large soft shell turtles and put it in a corn sack, and with the eggs in the paper sack, we proceeded to try out our plan. I climbed onto a stump with the turtle, and John rode the mustang to the stump and alighted, placing his hands over her eyes while I put the sacked turtle across the rear of the saddle just behind me. Then John remounted the horse, riding in front.

Everything worked out as planned until we had gone about a mile. The turtle began moving about in the sack, scratching the mustang in the flank. At that split second both of us found ourselves flat on the ground. By this time the mustang was halfway home, and we had to walk the rest of the way, taking turns carrying the turtle.

I think the horse suspicioned something was tricky when she saw me on the stump with the sack in my hands. We finally arrived at our home and killed the turtle, and my mother made turtle soup, which we enjoyed very much.

There were some ponds in the woods near where the road enters the Gulf sand dunes near where Four Mile Village is now located. We believed the Indians had dug the ditch running from the ponds to Horseshoe Bayou. This was done to catch fish after the water was lowered in the ponds. When visiting in that area in 1975 I was told by some residents that the ditch was still there, but they did not know that

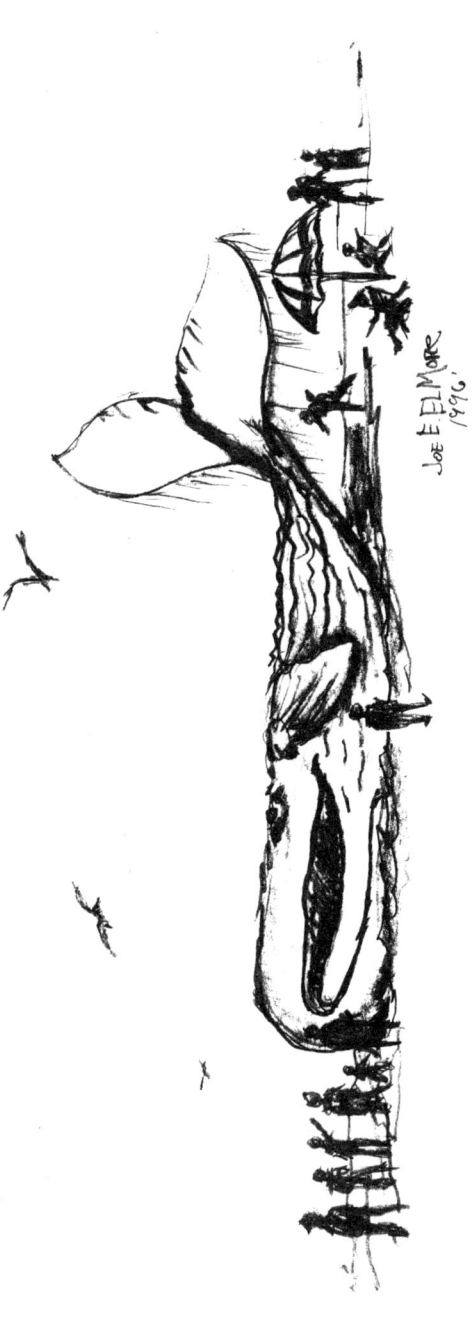

"…[W]hen we arrived on the beach we saw something down the beach and out in the water a short distance—something that looked like a wrecked ship…. As we grew nearer the object, the hair began to raise on our heads. When we were opposite it we could see the waves moving the forked tail about and we decided that it was a whale." Drawing by Joe E. Elmore.

the Indians had had anything to do with it. We always called it the Indian ditch.

John and I made another trip to the Gulf, but this time we each had a horse. We traveled the same road that we always used, and when we arrived on the beach we saw something down the beach and out in the water a short distance—something that looked like a wrecked ship. The horses began to act like they scented something and finally refused to go any farther. We took them over the sand dunes and tied them to a spruce pine and we walked to the object.

We both were barefooted, as we most always were in the summertime, and near the water's edge we ran into something oily that gummed up our toes and stuck to our feet. As we grew nearer the object, the hair began to raise on our heads. When we were opposite it we could see the waves moving the forked tail about and we decided that it was a whale. It was not dead but we judged that it must have been sick as there was no evidence of life as far as we could tell.

We hurried back home and told Mother about what we had found. She called my father in and we insisted that he ride over and see for himself. It took some time for us to convince him that we actually had found a whale, but he had to go over there to see for himself. When he came back he said it *was* a whale and a very large one, seventy-nine feet long. But the fishermen at Destin discovered him first. He went aground there and they tied a rope around his tail and tied the rope to a post they drove down in the ground, but he pulled the post down and drifted to the place where we found him.

The whale went to pieces and the bones washed ashore and lay in the hot sun until they bleached white as snow. Several months later the Bowers family from DeFuniak Springs were visiting us and we all went on a picnic on the beach. The skull of the whale was turned over and twelve of us ate our picnic lunch in the cavity of the skull. There was no odor about it as the sun had bleached it and it was a very dry bone.

A party from Pensacola towed a barge up into Horseshoe Bayou and came to our house asking if we could furnish them with a team of oxen to haul the skull over and load it on the barge. My brother Tilden took three yokes of our oxen and tried to haul the skull over to where the barge was, but it was too heavy and they had to give up and return without it. They said that it was their plan to unload it on to a flat car and have the railroad switch the car off at various places where they would charge admission to see it.

Several years later I was in Pensacola and stopped at the old Bay Hotel on South Palafox Street. In the lobby they had one of the fin bones and several of the teeth, which were about the size of bananas, but they never did get the skull off the Gulf beach.

Once I remember we had a game that would bring in lots of fun. Our home was often visited by people from other sections of the Bay and often there would be some boys that never had visited a place like ours. Our game was "snipe hunting," given this name in order to keep our victim from any suspicion. We would take our visitor out into the woods and when we came to one of the wild animal trails leading into a pond or swamp, we'd give him a sack and tell him to hold the sack open while we'd go around the pond or swamp and run the snipe down the trail and into the sack. Then we would go home, taking the dogs, and leave him holding the bag, and he didn't know the way back home. If he did manage to find his way, we'd tell him that he didn't carry out our instructions and we lost him.

Anything for amusement and fun suited us. We did lots of hunting at night for coons, possums, and fox. It was great fun to have several fox dogs chasing a fox and sometimes they would run him into our yard, but very seldom would they catch him. But coons and possums were different. The dogs could tree them and we would cut the tree down and let the dogs do the rest.

Sometimes friends from Freeport would come visiting us for a week or two. I remember once Dudley McCaskill came for a visit. He was about my age, both of us just learning how to shoot a shotgun. Once we were hunting a rabbit in the cornfield, when the corn was as high as our heads, and the dogs were on the chase. Dudley was at one end of the cornfield and I was at the other. While I was standing expecting to get off a shot, I heard something at my feet, and when I looked down I was almost astride a large rattlesnake. I fired both barrels at him just before he would have bitten me. We gave up our hunt for that day.

Chapter 8
Father's Civil War Stories

Aunt Eliza Bowers, who lived in DeFuniak Springs, had three daughters and one son. The daughters' names were Lee, Vida, and Myrtie, and son Wilson. My aunt, during the summer tourist season, operated a hotel at Grayton Beach, a resort over on the Gulf and about four miles from Point Washington. Brother John and I most always took off from our work about four weeks in the summer and we would spend that time out at Grayton Beach. We stayed with our aunt and helped out with the guests, showing them around the premises and taking them fishing, and helping Wilson with his large draft horse and wagon which had four seats on the body. We would meet the mail boat, the *Mayflower*, at the regular docking place on the bayou at Point Washington and take the passengers to my aunt's hotel at Grayton Beach. Sometimes we would have a wagon load. There was a beautiful lake near the Gulf and hotel, with plenty of fish in it and lots of clear, shallow water for bathing.

There was a family across the lake named Miller, who had some pretty daughters that liked to dance. Mr. Miller often gave a square dance and invited several people. Wilson was a fine fiddler and furnished the music. Of course we passed the hat around often to keep him from getting "tired." Sometimes we would dance all night.

I remember one night at the dance one of the guests attending, who was in the "golden age" group and did not have an escort, got tired of dancing. She lived on the opposite side of the lake and wanted someone to take her across the lake. Someone shouted out real loud and asked for a volunteer to take the lady home and brother John volunteered. He helped her into the boat and about halfway across the lake the boat

Grayton Beach—Circa 1890

Ladies in full-length dresses and parasols lounge on the blinding white sand at Grayton Beach, the oldest beach community in Northwest Florida. Courtesy, Van R. Butler, Sr.

Boyhood around the Choctawhatchee Bay

capsized and both, of course, were soaking wet. John said she blamed him for capsizing the boat and blessed him out, but he waded her ashore and went home.

Another time two young ladies from the North were guests at the hotel and wanted to go fishing in the Gulf. Brother John and I had a dory [a small, narrow, flat-bottomed fishing boat] that was easy to capsize. It was all fixed before we left the shore that it would capsize, so when we pushed the boat out into the breakers where the water was not too deep, as one of the girls could not swim, it flipped over and we all got wet. Again we were blamed for capsizing the boat, this time correctly. We returned the girls to the hotel. I will not call their names; they were real nice. We did not take them out in the boat anymore. John and I dated the young ladies several times while they were at the beach.

After our stint of helping at the hotel in Grayton Beach, John and I returned home to Mother's good cooking. She would serve all of us supper, and then we'd retire to the long front porch facing the Bay to hear my father tell some of his favorite Civil War stories about the fierce battles he was in. All of us, the family and any company we might have, would pull our chairs close to Father. The story for the night might be one that we had invariably heard him tell dozens of times, but it would be as new to us hearing him tell it as it was to him to tell it.

Before the Civil War, my father operated a sawmill on Piney Point which is at the mouth of Alaqua Bayou on the north side of the Choctawhatchee Bay. When he was called to serve in the organizing of the Walton Guards in Old Eucheeanna in Walton County, he closed down his mill and tied up one of his large schooners, the *Star of the West*. He donated the service of the other one, the *Lady of the Lake*, for transporting the newly organized recruits that had signed up in Eucheeanna to proceed to the selected camp site at what was subsequently called Camp Walton [now Fort Walton Beach] at the western end of Choctawhatchee Bay and on the narrow strip of water known as the Narrows.

There were less than a hundred recruits to start with, but the number increased as the training progressed. The *Lady of the Lake* was tied up at a place on Alaqua Creek and just south of Eucheeanna, and

Father, Captain Henry W. Reddick
Confederate Officer—Circa 1861

"[Mother] would serve all of us supper, and then we'd retire to the long front porch facing the Bay to hear my father tell some of his favorite Civil War stories about the fierce battles he was in. All of us, the family and any company we might have, would pull our chairs close to Father. The story for the night might be one that we had invariably heard him tell dozens of times, but it would be as new to us hearing him tell it as it was to him to tell it." [Henry Reddick's memoirs, *Seventy-Seven Years in Dixie: The Boys in Gray of '61 - '65*, was revised in 1999 by Coastal Heritage Preservation Foundation, a branch of South Walton Three Arts Alliance, Santa Rosa Beach, Florida.] Courtesy, Florida State Archives.

Boyhood around the Choctawhatchee Bay

her captain was my father's brother Madison. The recruits were marched aboard of the schooner and they sailed southward to the camp. Arriving there the next day they began erecting camping huts and tents—these living quarters were directly behind the large Indian mound, selected because of its invulnerability. [The Great Mound, built as a ceremonial and political center thousands of years ago, is the focal point of Fort Walton Beach's Indian Temple Mound Museum. Over four thousand artifacts of stone, bone, clay, and shell are exhibited here, along with historical information on the Confederate troops that camped on this site.]

It was only a short distance across Santa Rosa Island to the Gulf, and Union warships could easily drop shells on them if they knew their exact location. This did happen when their sentries were on guard. They detected a Union warship out in the Gulf and shortly after they made their report, the warship opened up fire with cannon balls dropping all about the camp.

My father was Second Lieutenant and in charge. He was asleep when they told him to get up because the Yankees were firing on them. My father thought it was a joke and was slow about getting out, but when a cannon ball tore off the top of his shanty, he then believed the report. He said that his men were running everywhere. Some of them swam Five Mile [now Cinco] Bayou and it took over a week to get them all back in camp.

In 1910 my father wrote and published a book, *Seventy-Seven Years in Dixie*, which has a clear and distinct account of all the events of his life in the Civil War and the battles he was in. He started to lose his eyesight when he began writing his Civil War memoirs, and sister Ida helped him on the first part of the book and I helped write the last part of it from his dictation.

The Union Army had destroyed his sawmill on Piney Point and had burned his two large sailing schooners down on the water's edge. They also drove off all of his large beef cattle and butchered them to help feed the Union Army.

Some evenings Father might tell us how dangerous it was to travel about alone in those days as there were still a few Indians hidden in the woods. He told about the Indians that would attack the stagecoaches between Marianna and old St. Joseph, Florida, which traveled through Tallahassee to a point on Apalachicola River, down the river to Lake Wimico, then on to St. Joe. He said they had to always have a guard along on the coach, with a gun in hand in case an attack was made. St. Joseph was then a small city, but I think it was the first capital of the state and was an important place. The yellow fever wiped it out.

The Disappearance of St. Joseph

THE FOUNDERS OF ST. JOSEPH, located one mile south of the present town of Port St. Joe, wanted to compete as a trading port with neighboring Apalachicola, which handled the Alabama and Georgia cotton traffic that floated goods down Apalachicola River to waiting ships in Apalachicola Bay. But St. Joseph Bay didn't have a river connecting it up North, prompting developers to build Florida's first steam-powered railroad. The line ran from St. Joseph to Lake Wimico, later being extended to Iola on the Apalachicola River, and opened for business in 1839.

According to Allen Morris's book, *Florida Place Names*, this bustling town was known as the "richest and wickedest" city in the southeast. Partly because of this distinction, St. Joseph was selected to host the convention that drafted the first Florida constitution in December 1838, although the town had been created only three years earlier.

For thirty-four days the elected delegates drafted their constitution until Friday, January 11, 1839, the question was asked, "Shall this be the Constitution of Florida?" Fifty-five ayes and one nay were heard. (It was six years later before the United States Congress admitted Florida into the Union.)

The shipping industry never took off, so St. Joseph, with its cool Gulf breezes, evolved into a resort town. Disaster struck in 1841 when yellow fever arrived. In less than a year the population had fallen to four hundred. Then in September 1844 a deadly hurricane and tidal wave swept the town clean, leaving only its over-populated cemetery.

When the storytelling came to an end, my dad would walk down to the Bay and take his bath, preparing himself for retiring for the night. There was a boardwalk from the porch to the Bay, and when he was walking on the boardwalk one night, I hid myself behind a rosebush. When he was passing I pulled the rattlesnake skin—John and I had killed and skinned and stuffed it with wheat bran—across the walk and he stepped on it and jumped sky high almost. I could not play this joke on him but one time, though, and after he had stepped on the snake I had to disappear until the next day. I was the only one in the family that could do this and get away with it.

Back in the early part of the twentieth century the Confederate veterans would hold annual reunions in the large cities of the South. The cities were glad to have the veterans' reunions as there were lots of them to begin with, and it always brought in much-needed revenue. My father always looked forward to attending these reunions as the veterans had much in common, and very often met some of their old friends who were in the same company and fought their battles together. There was much preparation made by the host cities and they tried very hard to make the old veterans enjoy themselves. I often went with my father to take care of him and I was afforded the same accommodations as he. The railroads would cut their rates to half-fare for the veterans and any of the family that went as caretakers, such as I was.

This occasion lasted many years until most all the large cities had made themselves host to the organization of Confederate veterans. The reunion attendance grew thinner each year. I think the last one that was held was with the Union veterans in some Southern city. I joined the Sons of the Confederacy in Memphis and I am still a member in good standing. My age is now eighty-seven.

During the fall of the year often we could see schools of mullet passing in front of our home. We could see the fins protruding above the water, and sharks and porpoise would be feeding among them—causing the fish to jump out of the water. I remember John and me rowing a skiff out among the school of mullet and some of them would jump into the boat. These mullet came into the Choctawhatchee Bay through the east pass at Destin and sharks would follow them in.

There were no large man-eating sharks in the Bay, but occasionally you could see a smaller species that we called shovel-nose type. They were not dangerous like the ones that followed the mullet.

There were several kinds of fish in the waters of the Bay while we lived on Four Mile Point. These were mullet, saltwater and freshwater trout, sheephead, flounder, and several kinds of bream. Of course, the freshwater trout and the bream were only caught in the bayous in fresh water. The flounder was the easiest one to catch, as he came in close to the shore to feed. The mullet was also easy to catch. They'd come in close in schools and we used the cast nets to throw over and catch large quantities of them, sometimes making only one cast to catch all that we wanted.

It was only two miles from our home to Eagle and Buck Bayous, and John and I would fish with hook and line to catch trout and bream. This was small-scale fishing. Over on the Gulf our older brothers and the boys that my father and mother took in would fish with seines and would catch bluefish, mackerel, and mullet.

There were two men I did not know who worked at the fishery. They had a small sailboat and kept it at the dock at the head of Horseshoe Bayou. One freezing cold day they headed the boat out into the Bay along with a large dog. A storm was coming our way and they did not get far before the boat capsized. One of the men stayed with the boat that was turned bottom side up by the turbulent weather. He held the dog in his arms and saved himself, also the dog. The body of the other man washed ashore nine days afterwards.

Fish was one of our main sources of food and the supply was unlimited. In season we would enjoy the fine oysters from Horseshoe Bayou. We used homemade tongs to gather them. No one knew who planted the oysters in the bayou. Some thought that they were put there by the Indians as there was plenty of evidence along the banks where my father built our home. There was a mound of shells near our backyard and some shells in our fields.

Chapter 9
Cowboy Days

There were no doctors closer than Point Washington, twenty miles away. Mother and Father had a doctor's book that was about three inches thick, and when any of us had any kind of ache, they would consult the book and make a diagnosis. They always kept a supply of calomel, quinine pills, and castor oil. [Calomel was used as a purgative medicine, quinine pills were used to treat malaria, and castor oil was used as a laxative.] If your ache was not relieved by taking one of these, then you kept taking them until the whole medical supply was exhausted! Usually all of us would keep our aches to ourselves and there were very few complaints among us.

I remember after supper on Saturday nights my father would go into the main house and return with a box of pills—rattling them in the box—after which all at the table would lose their appetites. All had to take a pill whether we needed it or not. Anyway it kept the doctor away.

I do not recall any of us having a bad cold. When it began to turn cold, my mother would make us put on our homemade red flannels and wear our shoes—this was a MUST. We were not allowed to quit wearing our red flannels until May 1—we could go barefooted then, also. By our following a few rules laid down by our parents, our health was usually very good.

I never saw my father sick but one time. That was when he and my mother were staying temporarily at the homestead near Santa Rosa. He was taken ill suddenly and none of their remedies would help him. I rode one of the horses up to Point Washington and got Dr. Lewis to drive down and see him, which he did. He stayed with us all day and night, and my father was some better and was soon up and going again.

REDDICK CEMETERY

Three markers and a wire fence around an unknown children's grave make up half of the Reddick family cemetery, still safely hidden amongst the piney woods west of Mack Bayou. Little Lucy McCormick, sister of Elizabeth Reddick, was the first person laid to rest, on March 2, 1872 (grave marker in the foreground). Born the same month the Civil War ended, Lucy was a month short of her seventh birthday. Her mother Emily was buried next to her (marker not shown) four short years later, living to the age of forty. The words on the grave markers of Millard and Jefferson Reddick (center), two of Elizabeth and Henry Reddick's children, still echo with a mother's grief:

SACRED TO THE MEMORY OF MILLARD F.
SON OF H. W. AND E. G. REDDICK
BORN DECEMBER 10, 1884-DIED JUNE 1, 1891

> Here sleeping peace a mother's joy,
> A mother's pride and darling boy.
> The living feels the blow,
> That so untimely laid him low.
> God, when the earthly race is run,
> Restore me to my darling son.

Kim Riegel Photography, Copyright © 1999.

SACRED TO THE MEMORY OF JEFFERSON MONROE REDDICK
SON OF H. W. AND E. G. REDDICK
BORN JULY 2, 1875-DIED SEPTEMBER 20, 1885

> God, know how hard it is to lay thee here with Him
> We leave Thee our infinite sacrifice of our golden haired boy.

Boyhood around the Choctawhatchee Bay

I had three brothers that died while we lived at Four Mile Point, Millard Fillmore, age six, and Jefferson Monroe, age ten, and, of course, baby Guy who was only five days old. All three are buried in the Reddick cemetery on the west side of Mack Bayou on Four Mile Point peninsula. I do not remember the passing of the two older brothers, but I do remember little Guy as I was seven years old. I helped my father make the small casket in which he was buried, and soon after, I built a picket fence around the grave and painted it white. The fence was still standing in August 1975, when three of my nieces took me down there.

For fun and pastime my two sisters, Ida and Jeannette, sometimes played jokes on some of the family. This time the joke was to be on sister Ellen Grace, who lived a short distance from our home. One of our fields then being prepared for cultivation was between our home and Ellen's. One hot summer day, while Ellen was alone with her young baby, my two sisters donned some of my older brothers' suits, blackened their faces, and went out in the woods in a direction where Ellen could not see them. They then proceeded towards Ellen's house, both armed with shotguns. Sister Ellen saw them coming towards her house, and as they came closer she took the baby under one arm and went out a side door and headed for our home. She was barefooted and the newly plowed ground was burning her feet. When she'd look around to see if Ida and Jeannette were gaining on her, she'd go a little faster because the two sisters would aim their guns on her. All this time the rest of the family was looking on from a china tree in our yard. Ellen was almost exhausted when she reached our home and Ida and Jeannette were close on her heels. It was a good joke on Ellen.

Upon another time a half brother was AWOL from the Navy, this being during the Spanish-American War, around 1898. We had at that time an old gentleman we called Uncle Billy (forgot his surname). Uncle Billy knew that officers were looking for the half brother and he was instructed, in case any officers came around inquiring about my brother, to tell them that he did not know anything about him or did not even know him. Ida and Jeannette, one of them dressed in my brother's navy uniform and the other in my brother's suit, approached Uncle Billy while he was plowing in the field. One of them had a gun and they asked him if he had seen my half brother around there at any time.

Uncle Billy told them that he had never heard of that man. They told him that they believed he did know where he was and threatened him if he didn't tell them the truth.

After they could not get Uncle Billy to give them the information, they went away. Uncle Billy went to the house to ask my mother if that was them durn girls fooling him. Of course, my mother told him the truth.

While I was at home and between schools, I was the cowboy. We had a large herd of cattle, including the offspring of my namesake's gift of the cow and calf. We always rounded up the herd in the spring. My mother and sisters would milch the ones that had calves, and, of course, all of them were put in the same pen. There would always be about twenty calves to separate from their mothers and turn out to feed in the woods at night. The next morning I would have to round them up and bring them to the pen. I always had help, though, a dog named Mack.

We had bells on two or three of the calves, and I would take Mack out a short distance, and he would listen for the sound of the bells. When he located the direction, he would go after them and run them in and would not leave any behind, either. Me being the cowboy, I had to saddle my favorite horse Sally and go for them. Sometimes they would be as far away as three or four miles but we would find them and Mack would see that we brought all of them in.

My favorite horse was a slender black mare. My father bought her from a racetrack operator in Walton County and they brought her over to Four Mile Point by schooner and dumped her overboard when they arrived in front of our house. Then she swam ashore. Brother John and I often saddled two of the horses and went out into the woods and had a horse race. Of course, my father did not know about this and would not have tolerated it.

Chapter 10
Dangerous Journey to Ione's

After the turn of the century, my mother and sister Jeannette were asked to take over and operate a hotel at Whitfield just across the Bay from our home on Four Mile Point. Whitfield was a sawmill town along Alaqua Creek. The mill was owned and operated by Mr. Harvey Berry and Mr. Henry Jernigan and sons. Their boarders were mostly the officials and skilled workers at the mill. Occasionally there were some traveling salesmen stopping overnight. My mother had some stables built in back of the hotel to take care of the salesmen's horses—I was the caretaker of the stables. I would take their horses and put them up in our stables and feed them for twenty-five cents per horse—most always a double team for which I would receive fifty cents for the care of two horses.

As I remember, my mother needed more help in the kitchen and with some of the housework. She knew of a good helper who lived at Point Washington and contacted her. Her name was Miss Lou Little and she started to work in the hotel. Lou was an uneducated person. A man named Williams—known as Professor Williams—was also uneducated. He operated a shoe repair shop on one of the sawdust roads in town not far from where Lou worked at the hotel. It was not very long before Lou and "Fess" struck up a very serious courtship. They were soon married, and I remember my mother and sister Jeannette gave them a nice reception after the wedding. Lou continued working at the hotel until my mother, after operating the hotel for about two years, decided to give it up and move back to our home on Four Mile Point. Father and brother John had stayed at home during my mother's absence to take care of the home and farm and also the stock.

Sister Jeannette and Mr. E. H. Jernigan, a member of the sawmill company, were married and lived on in Whitfield. I went back home with my mother, but later sister Jeannette wanted me to stay with them and go to school, and Mother and Father agreed for me to do this. The schoolhouse was about three miles in the country but the mill company furnished the lumber for a boardwalk out to the schoolhouse. It was a one-room house with a potbellied stove in the middle, and the stove pipe was down about as much as it was up.

Our teacher's name was Miss Crissie Gillis. Her home was in DeFuniak Springs. She was of the very famous family of Gillises that were pioneers of Walton County mentioned so many times in John L. McKinnon's book, *History of Walton County*. I can remember the names of most all of the students in the school. Mr. Charlie Brown lived just back of the school and he had several children. I remember two of them, Kathryn and Charles.

Sister Jeannette's house was small and they soon had an increase in their family. Inita was born while I was there, so they built an annex onto their home with two rooms upstairs. I occupied one of them with Wallace Campbell, a young man that worked in the company store with Jeannette's husband. I also helped some in the store.

The depth of Alaqua Creek was about twenty feet but it wasn't wide enough for a large schooner to turn around. It was four miles from the mouth of the creek, at the head of Alaqua Bayou, to Whitfield. Large steamer boats would unload freight on a platform at Mr. Henry Jernigan's large general merchandise store. But the steamers had to back out of the creek to the bayou before they could turn around on account of the creek being so narrow. Years before the Civil War there was a ferry where the bridge is now. The source of this creek was near the old town of Eucheeanna and just south of DeFuniak Springs. This is the same creek, Alaqua, that my father's schooner, *Lady of the Lake*, sailed the recruits down and into Choctawhatchee Bay to Camp Walton during the Civil War.

The lumber company's office was in the rear of the store building. Mr. Albert Jernigan was the store manager of the office, and they had a young man from Atlanta, whose name was Walter Wagner, as the stenographer. Walter taught me how to write on the typewriter. I think my brother-in-law still had the typewriter in his store in Quincy, Florida—I could be mistaken but it looked like it.

Mr. Albert taught me all he could about his work in the office, such as keeping books for a lumber company. This little push gave me the incentive and direction for my life's journey and I hope he realized this. With the knowledge which I kept all the years, I had the opportunity to attend Massey College when I was about sixteen years old.

We had a customer that lived about four miles from the store. He would buy a month's supply of groceries, and I would hitch up an old sloth-footed mule to the wagon and start out to make the delivery. There was a bridge over Alaqua Creek that I had to drive over on my way to the customer's home. The old mule was as stubborn as any mule could be. When we arrived at the bridge, he balked and would not budge. I beat him until I wore out the whip and realized that he did not intend to go on the bridge. So I got down off the wagon and took the bridle and jerked him around off the foot of the bridge, and he fell into the creek. The wagon did not go with him entirely, and he was about to drown. There was a small sawmill within hollering distance of me, and several of the men came and helped me get the mule out of the creek. He was now willing to cross the bridge when we got him hitched to the wagon. I didn't have any further trouble with the mule on that trip.

But some time later, Wallace Campbell and I had dates with two Portland ladies and we did not have our own transportation to travel the four miles to fill our dates. Wallace and I roomed together, and we planned to ease out one of the sawmill company's horses for Wallace, and I would take the old stubborn mule. We did so, saddled them, and started out to Portland. Both young ladies were in the same home so we didn't have to separate. When we arrived he hitched his horse to the picket fence and I tied the old mule to a pine tree.

After ten o'clock, which was the maximum check-out time, we went out to mount the horse and mule, but the mule had slipped his bridle and was gone. After looking around a while, I decided that the old stubborn thing had gone back to his stable. The road was wide and sandy with blackjack low bush on either side. I started out walking and looking—Wallace stayed with me, riding his horse. About halfway I heard some noises out in the bush. It was the old mule, but he would not let me get close to him, so I ran him all the way to the stable at Whitfield. We eased both the horse and mule in their stables without further mishap.

During my stay with sister Jeannette at Whitfield, I also attended a writing school and a singing school. I could never sing so my singing school did not ever accomplish anything.

While I was going to school in Whitfield, I met a sweet little girl by the name of Ione Campbell, Wallace's sister. She was about my age and we played together most every day and our friendship grew almost to the affectionate stage. Her mother and father ran the hotel—that was after my mother and sister ran it—and her father was a doctor. She had a sister named Annie and two more brothers named Charlie and Chipley.

Singing School

THE SINGING SCHOOLS of the late 1800s and early 1900s were among the few church- and family-approved recreations for young people in the community. Sacred harp singing was taught at these local singing schools. This method was designed so that untrained singers could learn to sight-read music. This style of singing is without musical instruments, but the voices make up for that lack with their volume, intensity, and enthusiasm.

The leader would usually place the singers in a square around him—the tenors ahead of him, altos seated to the rear, basses to the right, and trebles to the left. The page number and the verse would be called out and the pitch set by one person, by voice. Sacred harp music is written in shape notes which resemble the standard round ones except the head of each note has one of the four major shapes to indicate its interval from the key pitch. The four shape system is fa-triangle, so-oval, la-square, and mi-diamond. Before the words were sung, the tune would be sung in just the four notes.

"I built a small boat about six feet long, large enough to carry me. I completely rigged it up in every respect and carved the name 'Ione' on it in honor of my newly made friend.... I put it into the water and raised the sails and headed out for deep water.... My mother happened to see me out there in the Bay in that little thing, and she was awfully frightened, almost to death, and she waved something white, signaling me to return to the dock, which I did very quickly... I do not remember how many switches she wore out on me, but she put me on probation for several weeks." Drawing by Mary Ellen Brockett.

After I went back to our home on Four Mile Point, I missed my little friend very much. I built a small boat about six feet long, large enough to carry me. I completely rigged it up in every respect and carved the name "Ione" on it in honor of my newly made friend. After I had put the finishing touches on the little boat, I put it into the water and raised the sails and headed out for deep water. The wind began to get too strong for the small boat and it came near capsizing several times.

My mother happened to see me out there in the Bay in that little thing, and she was awfully frightened, almost to death, and she waved something white, signaling me to return to the dock, which I did very quickly. On my arrival and after I had lowered the sails and gone ashore, she met me on the front lawn and led me to a peach tree in the yard. I do not remember how many switches she wore out on me, but she put me on probation for several weeks.

Another thing that happened about the same time was more tragic. I had two nice young puppies that I liked very much. I wanted to get into the fishing business like my older brothers over on the Gulf. I built a nice little play boat, hollowed out of a piece of wood, and covered the deck with a thin board, leaving a hole in the deck to store the fish. I also built a nice cabin on the rear end of it. I used a pin hook and a piece of thread for a line attached to a small pole to catch the small fish that stayed around the dock, and I would store them in the hole under the deck. At night I would pull the boat out on the beach and leave it there for the next day's catch.

One morning the puppies found the boat and fish. They not only tore off the sails but they chewed off the deck and ate the fish. Of course, this made me furious, and as much as I loved the puppies, I wished that the fish they ate would kill both of them. Sure enough, the next morning I found both of my puppies dead not far from where the boat was.

Chapter 11
The Wesleys and the Stricklands

Here are a few interesting facts about two families in Point Washington—the Wesleys and the Stricklands. John Wesley was a Methodist minister and served the only Methodist church in the town as long as I attended school in Point Washington. He passed away some time before I finished my school days there and was first to be buried in the cemetery, which was not far from his residence and is now called the Wesley Cemetery.

Reverend Wesley's family consisted of eight sons—Stephen, William, Joseph, Charles, John, Marvin, Walter, and Cleveland. Cleveland was a friend of mine. We were about the same age and I remember spending many nights with him in his father's home.

As I remember, Mrs. Wesley was in ill health and Ida Davis was living with them and did all the housekeeping, washing and ironing, and cooking, besides attending to Mrs. Wesley. Ida Davis's parents were very nice and well-known, but died while she was quite young. She did not have much chance in life, but she did manage to work her way through Beeson's College in Meridian, Mississippi, and later she was married to my brother John. She majored in Bible while in college, and just before her death she gave her Bible to my mother. When Mother died, she gave the Bible to me and I still have it.

The Wesley story is a long one and I will not try to go into all the details, but I will say here that one of the Reverend Wesley's sons, Charles, married my sister Ida and another of his sons, Joseph, married Annie McDonald, who was a sister to my sister Etta's husband, Green McDonald.

Mr. Simeon Strickland, often called Mr. Sam, was a very good friend of my father. They were in the Civil War together and my father visited Mr. Sam often in his beautiful home at Point Washington. In one of the large rooms he had a well stocked grocery business and Father usually shopped for some grocery items needed at our home.

I heard my father say that while they were in the same company and on the eastern shore of the Tennessee River, they received orders to cross the river and engage the enemy on the other side. They had no bridges they could cross over, but they did build some pontoon floats. But in order to pull the pontoons across the river, it was necessary to get a rope to the other side and fastened to a tree. So their commanding officer called for a volunteer to swim the river. After each one looked at the other to see if anyone would volunteer, Mr. Simeon Strickland stepped forward. The soldiers were loaded on the pontoon floats and were able to successfully engage the enemy.

Mr. Sam was married two times and by his first wife he had four girls, Katie, Nettie, Ettie, and Ina; and three boys, John, Simeon, and Grover. Grover and I were friends and sometimes we would have a boxing match. He had some gloves and we had lots of fun. I also attended several enjoyable dances at the Strickland mansion. Of course, most all dances of that time were square dances.

Mr. Sam's oldest daughter, Katie, married William Wesley, a lumber baron. Mr. Strickland and Mr. Wesley were partners in the large sawmill at Point Washington. Charles Wesley, sister Ida's husband, was manager of the large commissary connected with the lumber business. The Wesley mansion is now known as Eden State Gardens.

After the sawmill burned several years after I left, there were no other industries there and the Wesley families had to look elsewhere for employment. Most of them moved to Mississippi, including my sister Ida and Charlie Wesley.

After I left the peninsula I did not hear what became of the William Wesley family until I read in one of the Atlanta papers the account of Miss Katie's death in 1953 and that her body was shipped to Point Washington for burial in the Wesley Cemetery.

I write the above for an introduction to the following story of my last school days in Point Washington High School. Knowing our family as they did, when they found out that I was to enter the school for my

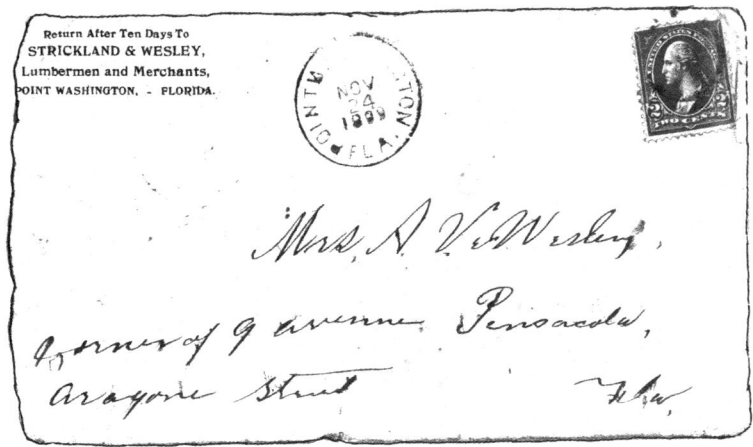

This letter was mailed on November 24, 1899, from the post office in Point Washington to Pensacola. Notice the return address from "Strickland & Wesley, Lumbermen and Merchants." Courtesy Ollie Sue Butler.

Miss Katie—Circa 1905

Katie Strickland Wesley asked the author's father if he could remain with the Wesley family in their home [the Wesley house is now known as the mansion at Eden State Gardens] while attending Point Washington High School. "Miss Katie, as we called Mrs. Wesley, assigned me to the southwest room upstairs.... I stayed in this room two years and was treated as one of the family."

last two years at Point Washington High School, Katie and William Wesley asked my father if I could remain with them during those last years.

After Father and Mother consulted with me, I decided to accept the offer, with my board being nominal. At that time the Wesleys had four children—Mabel, Rupert, Willie, and Guy. My mother got my clothes and school supplies together and took me up the week before school was to open. Miss Katie, as we called Mrs. Wesley, assigned me to the southwest room upstairs. The room was large with a nice bed, washstand, bowl and pitcher, and roomy closet. It also had a fireplace and wood container. (This same room now is called the Victoria Room.) My job would be to help Rupert, the oldest of the boys, bring wood and feed the cow and the fowls in the barnyard back of the house. They had a cook (I do not remember her name), also a housekeeper whose name was Miss Dora Lightfoot. She roomed just across the hall from me. I stayed in this room two years and was treated as one of the family.

While in school at Point Washington, I remember upon one occasion I was caught by a teacher passing notes to one of my favorite girlfriends through a torn place in a divider that separated two of the classrooms. When I saw the teacher coming my way, I put the note in my mouth and chewed it to pieces. The teacher demanded the note, but when I gave it to her she could not read it. She kept me in after school and gave me a good tongue-lashing and moved me to another location in the room. I now sat with another student, Homer Johnson, who became a very good and trusted friend. The teacher's name was Miss Payne—I called her Miss "Misery" afterwards. She was disliked by most all of the school.

We had another teacher named Mr. Pratt, who was the superintendent. We called him "Mr. Pratt could eat no fat" and we got in trouble about that. He happened to hear one of the boys calling him that one day, and the whole school was kept in that afternoon. He tried to get the guilty one to come forward and apologize but no one did. Mr. Pratt happened to be from the North—that might have been his trouble in getting along with the students. He was a good teacher but very strict.

It seems almost like a dream to recall some of the things that occurred in the Point Washington School. I believe if I were called on to name all the students that were in my room, I could do it. My favorite teacher in that school was Mr. Mitchner; he also was from the North. He was my math teacher.

My friend Grover Strickland decided that when school was out we would get into something and make some money. We had heard that a man named Mr. McAllily was buying cedar for a Chicago factory that manufactured pencils and cedar chests. We contacted Mr. McAllily in Freeport and found out that he was paying eight dollars per cord for cedar. Grover and I borrowed my father's large sloop boat and skiff—we also borrowed a crosscut saw and an ax from him, and then we were in business.

We first sailed about the Bay and bayous to locate the cedar. After we did this we began our work, first at a cedar hammock on Live Oak Point on the east side of the Bay. We had to cut a path through rush and mud to get a skiff into where the cedar was, and after we arrived at the island, we found it inhabited by all kinds of snakes. We took up quite a bit of time killing snakes, but we found lots of fine cedar there and cut most of it. Then we loaded it on the skiff and put it on board the sloop, which was anchored close by. We unloaded it at a landing on Buck Bayou. That was the first day's work.

The next day we went across the Bay to Basin Bayou, where we found more good cedar and loaded the sloop again. Of course, we had to anchor the sloop in deeper water outside of the bayou as the mouth (inlet) leading into the bayou was so narrow and shallow that we could not get the larger boat into it. We unloaded that day's cutting with the other that we had left on Buck Bayou. After we racked it up, we had almost five cords. At eight dollars per cord, we had made forty dollars already, which was lots of money in those days and especially for boys that were not used to having much money. You might ask if we had to buy the cedar. No, the people that owned the land did not want it growing on their land, so they would not have us pay anything for it.

We notified Mr. McAllily how much cedar we had and where it was on Buck Bayou. He dispatched his boat and crew and picked it up and gave us his check for it. The amount of the check was forty dollars, and

Grover Strickland—Circa 1900

"My friend Grover Strickland decided that when school was out we would get into something and make some money. We had heard that a man named Mr. McAllily was buying cedar for a Chicago factory that manufactured pencils and cedar chests. We contacted Mr. McAllily in Freeport and found out that he was paying eight dollars per cord for cedar. Grover and I borrowed my father's large sloop boat and skiff—we also borrowed a crosscut saw and an ax from him, and then we were in business."

we didn't have any overhead expenses except a few groceries since we cooked, ate, and slept on the boat.

Chapter 12
Living the Bachelor's Life in Santa Rosa

While staying with Miss Katie and Will Wesley, my mother sent me a pair of long pants. In those days a boy was a boy as long as he wore short pants, but when he put away his short pants and donned long ones, he was considered a young man, which was my position at that age. I remember making a date with one of the school girls to take her to the Baptist Church one Sunday. The church was about a mile and a half from where I was staying, and the young lady lived about a mile beyond the church, which made it about two and one-half miles to her home. The church services started at eleven o'clock. I put on my stiff shirt and the long pants and started out to pick up my date, but I was late and she had given me out and decided that she would go alone. So we met about half way from her home to the church. When I saw her coming I just knew that I would get a scolding, but I did not.

When we arrived at the church and went up the steps and into the main aisle, some of my schoolmates began to giggle and make fun. I was so excited and frustrated that we found ourselves down at the front on the first pew. I thought my long pants were what the gang was giggling about, and I also thought about this being my first date, all of which caused me and my date much embarrassment. After the services were over we started out the front door, and if there had been a back door, it would have suited us better to dodge that bunch of hecklers.

After the first year of high school, I went back home on Four Mile Point and worked with my father on the small farm and helped him with the cows and building fences. He had previously filed on a piece of government land, a homestead of about 160 acres, and built a small

Boyhood around the Choctawhatchee Bay

three-room house on it. The location of this homestead was about four miles south of Santa Rosa towards the Oyster Lake and extended back to Churchill Bayou on the Bay side. Father had to live a limited time on this land before he could get a title to it. Most of the land in the peninsula was U.S. Government land at that time.

After I returned to the last term of school staying with Miss Katie, my math teacher informed me that he was going to teach in Santa Rosa the next year. I decided that I would batch it at the homestead house of my father's and walk into Santa Rosa to school, because I was not satisfied with my advanced arithmetic, and Professor Mitchner was a very good math teacher.

I did this and walked into school Monday through Friday taking my lunch with me. There was a sawmill at Santa Rosa in the same location that my father's mill was once. I worked on the lumber yard loading boats with lumber at the McKenzie Lumber Company all day on Saturdays. And would you believe it, my pay was one dollar for my day's work. But that wasn't too bad. I saved that money and accumulated enough to pay my way to Noma, Florida, some time later.

This sawmill at Santa Rosa operated its own steam railroad and hauled its logs from several miles in the woods, and the train passed in front of the homestead house that I was batching in. Sometimes, when the train was on time early in the morning, I would catch a ride into school. It was a rough ride, as the track did not have a solid foundation and the ties would sink in the flat and wet woods. Once I was riding behind the tender [a railroad car attached to the rear of a locomotive, designed to carry fuel and water] and my straw hat caught on fire from the sparks from the locomotive, and I had to take it off and throw it into the woods.

I remember the inspector and foreman at the sawmill was Mr. Frank Gunn, whom I knew very well at Point Washington. His children—Arch, Ulysses, Ann, and Lilla—would pass my sister's house on their way to school at Point Washington. When I was staying with sister Etta, her children and I would join them. His family now ran the hotel at Santa Rosa.

While I was in school in Point Washington, I claimed one of the Gunn girls and was paying much attention to her. There was a man, the

Old Timers—Circa 1910

1—Will Wesley, owner of Wesley home, now known as the mansion at Eden State Gardens
2— Captain John Rogers, captain of *Captain Fritz* steamboat
3—Judge William Wilson, Santa Rosa's first postmaster and justice of the peace
5—Hartley Rutan, owner of general store in Freeport
4, 6, & 7—Unknown

Photo provided by the author.

Boyhood around the Choctawhatchee Bay

manager of the company commissary at Santa Rosa, I think his name was Bunkner, that had a large cigar in his mouth halfway down his throat. He was now going with the Gunn girl that I had claimed years earlier. But I didn't make any protest because the Gunn family had a relative of theirs visiting them from Gordon, Alabama, whose name was Miss Mae Coe. She was petite and very pretty, and I dated her and let Mr. Bunkner have the old friend of mine. Miss Coe and I carried on a very lengthy correspondence after she returned to Alabama.

At the end of the school, after I had finished my math course, I returned to our home on Four Mile Point. My half brother Will was living in the house that Mr. Thaggard had lived in at the turpentine still four miles east of our home. Mr. Thaggard and Mr. Junie Richardson, the owners of the still, had dissolved the business and all of the employees had moved away, leaving all the houses for anyone to move into. Will and I built a boat on the bluff near our home and skidded it into the Bay when we had finished. Then we cut and hauled cross-ties to Santa Rosa for the railroad which badly needed them. After we terminated this job, Will and his wife Amanda and two small boys moved to Mississippi, and I returned home again and worked with my father.

A very good friend, Adolphus Thomason, and I began a business of our own, independent from my father's timber business. We rented a team of three yokes of oxen and made an agreement with Father that we would pay him stumpage for each log we cut. We secured a tent and selected as our camping place a spot south of Mack Bayou near its tributary. We stored our groceries in one of my mother's large turtle-back trunks and did our own cooking.

We got our camping outfit set up and every other thing organized, then we began cutting the timber. After we had cut what we thought was a good-sized raft, we got the team of oxen and log cart and began hauling the logs to a tributary of Mack Bayou about half a mile from where the creek emptied into the bayou.

After we had hauled all the timber that we'd cut to the banks of the stream, we had to wait for a hard rain to swell the stream so we could float them to the bayou. We succeeded in getting them into the bayou and assembled all of them together in a raft with boom—a line of connected floating timbers around the logs to hold them together. Then we had to wait for a good stiff southwest wind to tow the raft across the Bay to a sawmill, with a sailboat we also borrowed from my father. We managed to get two rafts across the Bay without mishap. This adventure was a great success—luck was with us.

Father decided that he would get Adolphus and me to cut and haul some timber that he had bought from the defunct Turpentine Enterprises near the old Thaggard turpentine still and in the vicinity of Waldrops Creek, a tributary of Hewett Bayou. We took the job and cut and hauled the logs to the creek and floated them down to Hewett Bayou.

While we were doing this we had to be in the water up to our necks. In some mysterious way a fish got into my pants, and I thought it might be a snake because there were plenty of them there, but Adolphus helped me get the fish out. Then we proceeded pulling the logs together into a boom. We then waited for a good wind to sail them across the Bay to the sawmill. We were again successful in finishing the job for my father.

During school days at Point Washington several of us boys, after school on one Friday afternoon, decided that we would take a short vacation. One of the boy's fathers had a sloop, a boat with mainsail and jib, and we borrowed this boat and decided we would explore the Choctawhatchee River, which was only a short distance from Point Washington. We reached the river and sailed up it for a short distance when one of the boys suggested that we take off our clothes and dive off the boat into the river.

The water in the river was dark with the movement of the swift current, which brought all kinds of debris and an occasional submerged log. The water was beginning to get warm from the hot sun. One of the boys, Frank Mills, was the first to get his clothes off and climbed up on top of the cabin and took a dive. He did not come up to the surface of the water. We made probes with a pole and located a log that was about two feet under the water, but Frank did not come up.

We rushed back on the boat to Point Washington and gave the alarm. Several men, including his father, went back with us to the place where Frank took his dive but the body could not be located. Nine days

Boyhood around the Choctawhatchee Bay

after this happening they found Frank's body tangled up with brush and debris on one side of the river. All of the boys were like ducks in the water, but this taught us a lesson—never dive off into dark waters.

Sometime before the Choctawhatchee River accident, I was working in Freeport's King-Mayo large store. Most every Saturday night after closing the store, Homer Johnson and I would go down to Four Mile Creek about a block from the main street of the town and dive off into the dark waters of the creek. Luckily we did not dive into a log. I would never do it again.

My father and I camped on his large sloop and picked up sunken logs in Mack, Hewett, Campbell, and Churchill Bayous. These sunken logs were heavy with tar and had sunk to the bottom when rolled into the water when the land was logged. As it took too much time to raise a sunken log and belt it up to the rest of the raft, it was left to rest on the bottom of the bayou. So Father and I would build floats about fifteen feet long and about three feet wide, caulk and pitch the seams to stop leakage, then cut pine sapling poles about twenty feet long. We would lay them across the top of the float, the float being in the middle, then with a set of hooks around the sunken log we would bring it to the top and tie both ends to the stringer poles on the float. When we had about thirty of these floats fully loaded we placed a boom around them and sailed the raft across the Bay to a sawmill.

Chapter 13
1905 Yellow Fever Outbreak

There came a time at the age of fifteen that I had to decide what kind of a career I should adopt. I had mentioned to my parents that I wanted to make my own money to embark on the trip that I had made up my mind to make. I talked this matter over with them and they agreed that their youngest son should have the choice of his own career, although my leaving them would be their disadvantage in that their lives would be spent with much loneliness.

My father saw an advertisement in a magazine of a one-man folding cross saw. It weighed about sixty-five pounds. He asked me if I thought I could use it in cutting a schooner-load of cord wood. He ordered the saw and I went to work out in the woods. After falling a log, I would carry the heavy saw on my shoulder to the next tree. It took me about two months to cut what I thought was a schooner-load—about twenty cords. I borrowed a yoke of oxen and a wagon from my father and hauled the wood to a place on the west side of the peninsula of Four Mile Point convenient to float it out to the boat.

After I had all of the wood hauled, I got in touch with a cousin, Will Reddick, to come, and with my help, loaded it on his schooner *Synthia Jane* to sell it to the Gull Point Tar Plant up on Escambia Bay north of Pensacola. My mother had all my clothes laundered and packed in my suitcase ready to take aboard with me. I was leaving home on the same boat with my tar wood to take my trip.

After we had the boat loaded we set sail facing a very heavy west wind. We had to make tacks all the way to the quarantine station at the west end of the Santa Rosa Sound. When we reached the deep water there, the seas were running very high and the wind was very stiff and the boat began to take on water from the waves washing over the deck. Our hand pump became jammed and we had to let the boat drift over to the Santa Rosa Island side, dragging both anchors. I sat on the stern rail with the skiff line in my hands ready to get into the skiff in case the boat began to sink. We were so close to the island that I think I could have jumped to safety should the boat have started to sink. After the wind subsided we set sail and proceeded to the tar plant, unloaded the boat, and sailed back to Pensacola.

Will went uptown with me and I purchased some new clothes for my trip by railroad to my sister Ida's home in Howison, Mississippi. On arriving in Pensacola I discovered that yellow fever had broken out in town and in other Gulf coast cities. I was advised at the Louisville and Nashville Railroad station that most all points to New Orleans were quarantined and I would be taking chances of not getting through at that time. [To follow Mr. Reddick's travels consult the map on pages 108-109.]

I decided to take the chance. I boarded the train at Pensacola for Gulfport, Mississippi. I noticed when we arrived in Mobile that the police met the train and would check passengers' health certificates as they alighted, allowing them to leave the train. There I was without any identification to show that I had not been exposed to yellow fever. My chances of getting by the police at Gulfport when we arrived were very doubtful. Not so, though, because I got lost in the crowd and was overlooked by the police.

It was late in the evening when I checked in at a hotel which was close to the railroad station. I was informed by the hotel clerk, when he noticed that I was from Pensacola, that they had a suspicious case of yellow fever in that hotel and he doubted that they would let me off the train when it stopped at Howison, only twenty-one miles north. The train was due to leave Gulfport about six-thirty the next morning. At five-thirty I was up and dressed to go to the depot. When I arrived there I ordered a cup of coffee and a sandwich; I drank the coffee and took the sandwich with me on the train. When I arrived in Howison I was met by my sister Ida. There was a policeman there too, but sister

Brother
John H. Reddick

Brother
H. Tilden Reddick

Half brother
M. Lafayette O'Neal

Grandfather
William McCormick
Circa 1890

Photos provided by the author.

Ida told him that I had not been exposed to yellow fever and he didn't ask me any questions.

I was at sister Ida's home only a short time before I discovered that I had a high temperature. Sister Ida called Dr. McKnab, and after he had questioned me at length as to where I had spent the night before and had given me a thorough examination, he diagnosed my case as a suspicious case of yellow fever. He had the house quarantined and a yellow flag posted on the front of the house.

I knew that I had not been in contact with anyone that had yellow fever and told sister Ida to see if she could get another doctor. She telephoned McHenry, Mississippi, a small town three miles north of Howison, and contacted Dr. McHenry. She explained my case to him, and he came and examined me and pronounced it a bad case of typhoid fever. He had the yellow flags removed, put me to bed, and told me to stay there, and said he would come to see me once each day. This he did; I was there twenty-six days and lived entirely on something called "beef preparation." During this time my sister Ida wrote my mother and told her that I was very sick.

It was very difficult for my mother to get to DeFuniak Springs and get a health certificate, but with all this inconvenience, she went through with it. Dr. Henry of DeFuniak gave her the necessary health papers to convince the health officers that she had not been exposed to yellow fever. Each day they would tighten up on their travel restrictions, but my mother made the trip without mishap. She found me very sick, but she knew what to do in my case and within a few days I became much better, so much so that they let the doctor go.

I was soon up and walking some but very weak. My half brother Will lived at Caesar, Mississippi, about twenty miles to the west and near the great Pearl River Swamp. We hadn't seen him in a long time, so Mother wrote him that she was at Howison with her daughter Ida and would like to see him while she was so close.

The letter soon reached Will, and he and his wife Amanda came over in a one-horse surrey to take both of us back with them. The next morning we started out, traveling over the worst road I think I ever saw and through some of the finest pine I ever saw. We finally reached Will's home and he told me that there were plenty of squirrels and turkeys in the swamp. He had a gun and a dog. After I was over the long trip, although I was weakened from my recent illness, I decided that I would try killing some squirrels and probably a turkey.

There was an old wagon road which didn't go to the river but ended a short distance from where I went into the swamp. The dog stayed with me for a while but left me, and I did not see him anymore. Soon there came up a real dark cloud that looked very much like a tornado might be in the making. It soon began to rain and the water began to appear most all around me. I was lost and could not find my way back to the road where I went into the swamp. Neither could I find my way to the outer edge of the swamp. I began hollering as loud as I could and kept traveling, in what direction I did not know. I also fired the gun as long as I had shells.

By this time it was night and real dark. I came to a stream about twenty feet across and an old tree had fallen across it but it did not reach far enough. So I pitched the gun as far as I could to the other side and swam across, retrieved the gun, and began hollering again. I soon heard a faint answer. I kept going in the direction of the voice. I could see a fire ahead and was soon to the place. Mr. Breland was operating a grist mill there and had me come in the house and dry my clothes by the fire. After this he put me on a road which took me back to Will's house—it was eight miles but I kept going. It was good daylight and my mother was almost in a state of shock. She knew that I might relapse with typhoid fever from the ordeal, but after I was over it and had a few days' rest, Will took us back to Howison. Mother took the train back to DeFuniak Springs and on to our home on Four Mile Point, and I stayed on at Howison.

My sister Ida's husband, Charles Wesley, and two of his brothers, Joseph and Walter, operated the shingle and stave mill at the large lumber mill, the Native Lumber Company. They needed help and hired me. I worked with them for several weeks when a young man (I cannot recall his name) asked if I would be interested in joining him in partnership in leasing a shingle and stave mill one-and-a-half miles north of Howison and near McHenry.

I thought we might do well up there so we leased the mill and started operation. The first day I was bolting the timber into blocks while he ran the blocks through the shingle machine and a young man downstairs stacked the shingles into bundles. We were not operating long before my partner touched me on the shoulder and I looked around. He had four of his fingers cut off, including part of the upper hand. I closed down the machinery and took him into McHenry and had a doctor dress the wounded hand. But he was a very sick man and had to get to a place where he could get doctors' attention and nursing care. I took him to his home in Howison and his father and mother took charge of my patient.

By this time yellow fever in the coast towns was getting scattered and more travel restrictions were evident. You could go into one of the affected cities, but you were not permitted to leave.

I had made up my mind to try and get through to Pensacola or some other place near home. A doctor and his daughter were visiting relatives in Howison. He found out that I wanted to return home, or to Pensacola, and his home was Milton, Florida, near Pensacola. He told me that he had been told that by going through Hattiesburg, Mississippi, and Atlanta, there was a way open for travel to Pensacola or DeFuniak Springs. I said, "Yes, I would like to travel with you." I had heard from Mother after she arrived at Aunt Eliza Bowers in DeFuniak Springs and she had not been held up any place.

The good doctor and daughter and I bought tickets to Hattiesburg and boarded the Gulf and Ship Island Railroad train at Howison. The conductor came through, taking up tickets, and advised each passenger that when we arrived in Hattiesburg, we would be detained there until the quarantine was lifted. This upset me because I was running a temperature and did not care to get that far away from my sister Ida's home in Howison. I talked this over with the doctor and he advised me to return to Howison if I could make it. All three of us decided as we were approaching Wiggins that we would get off the train there and spend the night and get more information about the Hattiesburg quarantine. We stopped at a hotel near the railroad station. I was sick all night and when daylight came I told the doctor that I was going uptown to see if I could get someone to drive me back to a small station called India. I did contact a delivery stable that had a fast team of horses and the driver said he could put me on the southbound train.

That train was due in India in two hours and it was four miles to drive. I returned to the hotel and told the doctor that I had conveyance to India and had decided it would be best for me to return to Howison, and he agreed. I did catch the train back, and when I arrived at my sister's I was really sick—temperature very high. She called Dr. McHenry and he said I had a relapse of typhoid fever and I had it all over again for twenty days. This made forty-six days that I was sick.

Chapter 14
Oyster Dredging in Biloxi

After I missed my fever and was strong enough, I made up my mind again to return home. Like the Prodigal Son, I really wanted to go home. My cash was running low and I had to get into something quickly. I bought a ticket to Biloxi, and on arrival I went to the docks near the oyster packing and canning plant. I talked to some of the oyster fishermen about the prospects of going out on the oyster bars as a crew member and helper. I told them about the experience I had with boating and they said yes. I thought all the time that I was talking to these men that I recognized their faces and finally the captain of the boat *Canary* said his name was Noel Davis. I said, "Where are you from, Mr. Davis?"

He said, "I'm from Choctawhatchee Bay." Then I realized that I knew him and his brother Henry, who was one of the crew on the boat. Also with them was a man named DeShazo from Esto, Florida. There were two more men in the crew and a chef. The two Davis men were brothers to Ida Davis, the young lady who was the housekeeper for the Reverend Wesley and later married brother John.

After the schooner *Canary* was fitted with oyster dredges and windlasses and all the grocery supplies were aboard, we set sail for the oyster bars in the Mississippi sounds. Before leaving the canning plant, we were warned about some restricted bars that were being used by the U.S. Government for experimental purposes. If we were caught dredging for oysters on these particular bars—which were staked out and identified by flags flying from the tops of poles at each corner—we would be prosecuted. We advised the canning plant that we would do our best to abide by these restrictions.

Biloxi's oyster harvest was featured on the cover of *Scientific America* magazine in 1918. Dock workers are hoisting a basket-full of oysters from the schooner, unloading the day's work. Courtesy, Biloxi Public Library.

When we arrived at the place where we would begin our work of dredging oysters, we found what looked like thousands of other sailboats doing the same thing. They were so thick out there that sometimes the boats would run together. In some cases this caused damage to the vessels, which in some cases precipitated a free-for-all fight. But in all cases the matter of damage was settled judiciously.

My sleeping quarters were in one of the compartments in the forecastle. But I was informed before we began dredging that I would not need any place to sleep as we would be working all the time. I found that to be so because the boat, propelled entirely by sail and wind, had to pull the dredges to fill them full of oysters. So while the wind was blowing we would fill the deck of the boat with oysters, and when the wind was not blowing we would keep busy culling the small oysters that were under three inches long and throw them back into the water—this was government regulation. This kept us busy most all the time with no time for sleep.

Often we would have a government inspector come aboard and make inspections, and if we were caught with any oysters three inches long or less we would be subject to a fine. We were extremely lucky though as we didn't have any fights with other boatmen or have any fines for having on hand any of the small oysters.

In our grocery supplies we had two barrels of hardtacks. You may not know what a hardtack is; it is a piece of flour dough made up with water and some salt and when it goes through the baking process it is as hard as a rock. But if you were hungry enough, which all were most of the time, after working all night, you would be delighted to have two or three of them with a cup of strong coffee. This hardtack eating operation was started about the first signs of darkness, and our chef, with the galley on deck and plenty of hot charcoals, would have our coffee hot and plenty strong ready to serve all of us. This same hour of the day with hardtack and coffee was true with all the boats on the sound, and when the ovens were lit up it gave the appearance of a large city fully lighted on a dark night.

The Hidenham Canning Company of Biloxi, which owned the schooner *Canary* that we had leased, also owned a large three-masted schooner that would come out on the sounds and pick up oysters from boats that were loaded and take them back to the canning plant. Also, it brought groceries to boats whose crew had placed orders for them. The name of the large freighter was the *Baldwin* and the captain of the *Baldwin* would give a receipt for the oysters he picked up and carried to the canning plant, and we could cash the receipts in after the oyster season was over, when we returned to Biloxi. This arrangement with the supply boat bringing our supplies and picking up our oysters saved us much time and extra work.

During the time we were out between Cat Island and Deer Island there came a storm that almost wrecked our boat and did damage to some of our sails. We had to sail into Bay St. Louis through the Louisville and Nashville Railroad drawbridge and remain in the Bay for four days, patching sails and making other repairs to the boat, after which we returned to the bars. We were out there September through April—eight months without going ashore. [All the months with an "r" in their names are said to have good oysters.]

When we were through at the end of the season, we returned to Biloxi, cashed in our oyster receipts, and all went uptown to one of the best restaurants and each ordered a thick steak with plenty of Louisiana Hot Pepper Sauce. When we returned to the *Canary* our chef had prepared an oyster jambalaya and all of us ate so much that it made some of the men sick. They were sprawled out on the deck when I tried to tell them goodbye before catching the train for Pensacola. When I arrived in Pensacola, I went to Palafox Street wharf to see if there was a boat leaving for Choctawhatchee Bay. I found cousin Will Reddick who was fixing to set sail, and he was glad to have me go along.

Around this time, Lafayette and I began looking around for permanent employment away from Choctawhatchee Bay. His wife Bell had two brothers working in Noma, Holmes County, Florida, in a large sawmill—The Alabama and Florida Lumber Company. Her oldest brother's name was Pip Pippin—he was the sawyer at the mill. Pip and his brother Walter for some time had been encouraging Bell and Lafayette to move to Noma. The two Pippin brothers felt sure that a job at the large mill would be permanent, as the mill company had timber in sight to run the mill for quite a while. Lafayette talked to me about leaving the area and going to Noma, getting a job at the mill, and, if we liked it, moving his family there.

We went to Pensacola with brother Tilden on his schooner *Evelyn* and boarded the Louisville and Nashville Railroad train, made a change to another train at Crestview, Florida, to Florala, Alabama, thence by Central of Georgia Railroad train to Samson, Alabama, where we had to change trains to Louisville and Nashville Railroad for our destination—Noma.

We spent the first night with the Pippins. The next morning we went to the mill and contacted Mr. Marion Turner, the mill foreman, who had been informed that Lafayette would report for employment at the mill. Mr. Turner told us to come back the following morning and he'd put us to work. We did and he gave Lafayette a job in the planing mill and took me out on the lumber yard where almost all the stacks of lumber were twenty feet high. There was a push car track between these stacks of lumber, leading from the upper story of the mill and extending out to the end of the lumber yard.

The lumber would be loaded on the push car in tiers according to grades in the mill and then pushed out to the various stacks of lumber. Each grade was thrown off at the proper stack to which it belonged. I was instructed by Mr. Turner that my job was to place each board in its proper place on the various stacks. A two-by-ten-inch piece of timber was place from one stack to the other to walk across on. This was done because the lumber was stacked too far from the car track to step across and walk from stack to stack.

I worked on this job for about two weeks, when one day I started across on one of the two-by-ten-inch planks and one plank slipped off. Down to the ground both of us went, the plank falling across my right knee. Two men with a stretcher were called to the scene and they took me to the company doctor's office not far away. Dr. Warren was amputating a man's finger when they took me in his office. He examined me and said it would take me two weeks before I could return to work. I decided the work was too dangerous for me, and when I was able to travel I headed back home on Four Mile Point.

Chapter 15
Selling the Family Land

When Tilden married Miss Edna Senterfit of Portland, Father gave them several acres of land near our home. I helped Tilden cut some timber and we rafted it in the Bay and sailed it to the sawmill on the opposite side. He had it sawed into lumber and I helped him build his house on the land my father gave him.

The next year Lafayette and his wife Bell returned to Florida and homesteaded a piece of government land, 120 acres at the head of Horseshoe Bayou. His home was on the first sand dune where Mr. Thomas, one-time postmaster, had lived years before. Lafayette used some of the Thomas house lumber and material to build his home. Some of the letter boxes were still in the old house along with other evidence a post office had been there.

Lafayette and I were always looking for something to do to make some money. We cut and hauled a schooner-load of tar wood from his property to a landing on the west side of the peninsula. Brother Tilden helped us load the wood on his schooner, which carried it to the tar plant at Gull Point several miles up Escambia Bay from Pensacola. Lafayette and I also cut and hauled a boat load of tar wood from my father's homestead and loaded brother Tilden's boat with it on Churchill Bayou. He again delivered it to the tar plant at Gull Point. Between farming seasons, he and I started cutting cross-ties for the small railroad (log train) at Santa Rosa.

Lafayette moved his family to his homestead, bought a mule, and started to farm. The first year he only broke up enough land between his home and the head of Horseshoe Bayou to plant a patch of sugar cane. I was not there when the family was grinding cane and making syrup but I have a small picture of the event. In the picture was my Aunt Eliza Bowers and several other people helping Lafayette and Bell make the syrup.

My Aunt Eliza decided that she would homestead a 120-acre piece of government land just a few miles west of Lafayette's homestead. The location was where the Sun 'N Sand Motel is located on the Gulf [on Old Highway 98-now Scenic Gulf Drive] and reached back into the woods toward Choctawhatchee Bay. She lived on the homestead off and on for seven years after which time she received title to the land. She kept it for a few years and then sold it—I do not know to whom.

When I was a boy, brother John and I would ride down the peninsula to the high sand dune and climb on top of it and look for vessels in the Gulf. There was a yellow streak in the side of the dune and we always called it the "yellow bluff." I spent two nights in the Sun 'N Sand Motel in August 1975 and I told the motel operator that I had lots of fun playing on top of that dune and he was surprised. Of course, they had leveled the dune down considerably in building the motel.

My knowledge of the beginning and building of the community of Santa Rosa, Washington County, Florida, is that I was born and reared in the area and was living with my parents at that time on Four Mile Point peninsula west of Santa Rosa. We were familiar with the lands that Dr. Charles E. Cessna, developer from Chicago, purchased east of our home on Four Mile Point and to my knowledge the acreage was around thirty-five thousand. I do not know the exact price Dr. Cessna paid for the land, but I was told that it was close to $1.75 per acre. It was not unusual for undeveloped land to sell for this nominal price in that area at that time.

Soon after Dr. Cessna purchased the large acreage of land and after surveys were made and maps drawn, his agents soon recognized that the Henry W. Reddicks had a nice orange grove on their land on Four Mile Point, which would be a very valuable key to making sales to prospective buyers. When our orange trees were in full-ripe fruit, Dr. Cessna's agents made photographs of the grove and made prominent displays in their advertising brochures they mailed out to potential buyers.

Lafayette O'Neal Grinding Cane at His Mill—Circa 1905

"Lafayette moved his family to his homestead, bought a mule, and started to farm. The first year he only broke up enough land between his home and the head of Horseshoe Bayou to plant a patch of sugar cane. I was not there when the family was grinding cane and making syrup but I have a small picture of the event. In the picture was my Aunt Eliza Bowers and several other people helping Lafayette and Bell make the syrup." Photo provided by the author.

Boyhood around the Choctawhatchee Bay

The Cessna developers purchased, or had built, a large three-deck sidewheeler steamboat in Pensacola to bring land buyers into Santa Rosa. The agents of the developers would meet the trains in Pensacola and put them aboard the steamboat *Charles E. Cessna* and unload them at Santa Rosa. People of almost all nationalities usually were in each load. I believe the steamboat *Captain Fritz* handled the freight and passengers to Santa Rosa before the *Charles E. Cessna* came into existence. The bayou where the passengers and freight were unloaded was named Mill Bayou. It got its name when my father had his sawmill there after the Civil War.

My father still owned the 160-acre homestead out about four miles from Santa Rosa where I batched. At that time there were only a few families living there and one small commissary, a hotel, and the small schoolhouse where Mr. Mitchner taught me advanced math.

Mr. Lum Coran was one of the pioneers of the area who lived just a few miles north of Santa Rosa on the northern coast of Live Oak Point. He owned a piece of land similar to my father's on Four Mile Point, with Indian oyster shell mounds and a subsoil of soft brown rock foundation, which made good farming land. He raised most anything he wanted to plant, including watermelons. He and my father were competitors in this field, always trying to have ripe melons on the market first.

However, this kind of land was not prevalent in the peninsula area. Most of the land on the Cessna tract was either sandy loam or low flat woodland, and during the summer months it became somewhat soft and muddy due to the coastal showers during the planting season. The low woodland sometimes caused sour fungus and nematodes in the heat of the sun, which caused the roots of the plant to curl into balls and eventually die, so it was our experience that this kind of soil was not adaptable for farming. However, with proper drainage in the lowlands and fertilization in the sandy sections, some varieties of fruit trees and scuppernong vineyards might be grown profitably. It is highly possible that this could have been one of the downfalls of the community of Santa Rosa that left so many people stranded there.

Mr. McCaskill of Freeport pioneered the sale of the lands to Dr. Cessna. Mr. McCaskill had with him his head bookkeeper, Judge

William Wilson, who was the first postmaster of Santa Rosa. The McCaskills were sawmilling people [Choctawhatchee Lumber Company] on the LaGrange Bayou near Beatrice Point, the waterway to Freeport. They owned a large department store in Freeport, too. Judge William Wilson was also justice of the peace. That is when he received his title "judge."

When the steamboats began to bring in land buyers, the agents of the Santa Rosa Plantation Company took them out into the woods and let them select plots of ten, twenty, or forty acres. Small houses began to be built and the property fenced in with barbed wire and the whole operation began to take shape. On the Bay-front, prize lots were sold almost immediately and fine houses erected.

This operation began to spread down our way on Four Mile Point. One day in 1910 my father said that we were not used to having so many foreign people around and having to go around wire fences to get to other places, so he decided to make the newly formed land company a proposition for us to sell out to them, which he did. They accepted the price [$4331 was listed in the deed] for our home, land, and improvements as well as the homestead previously mentioned near Santa Rosa.

My father was informed that the agreement would be drawn up by the Santa Rosa Plantation Company by their attorney in the San Carlos Hotel in Pensacola and for him, my father, to appear there and sign the papers. Lafayette, who was living on his homestead at the Horseshoe Bayou at that time, took our horse and buggy and carried my father and me to Destin. A good friend of my father, Billy Marler, was postmaster at Destin at that time and I think we spent the night with him. The following morning we took a launch, the mail boat, to Pensacola.

On our arrival in Pensacola, we went to the San Carlos Hotel on North Palafox Street and contacted the attorney, Mr. Arthur Gammage, who already had the agreement made out for my father to sign. After that we started back to our home on Four Mile Point. We were instructed by Attorney Gammage to appear in Santa Rosa on a certain date to sign the deeds and receive the money for the property. My father, mother, Tilden, John, and myself executed the papers. [The deed was signed January 9, 1911.]

The Beginning and Ending of Santa Rosa Plantation

DR. CHARLES CESSNA, a physician and land developer from Chicago, purchased thousands and thousands of acres of land in 1909 along Hogtown Bayou (which he renamed Santa Rosa Bayou) and created a new town named Santa Rosa Plantation. He advertised heavily throughout the Great Lakes region touting a virtual paradise—few snakes and insects and near perfect temperatures. As many as twelve hundred people took the chance to try agriculture as a way of making a living—planting acres of scuppernong vineyards and orange groves. In 1915 citrus canker infestation caused the State Plant Board to call for thousands of orange trees to be destroyed, causing irreparable harm to the agricultural industry. The final blow came with the hurricane of 1926 when the sugar cane fields were swamped with brackish water. The town, which boasted three churches, two hotels, warehouses, post office, school, cannery, ice house, lumbermill, two turpentine stills, and two general stores, nearly became a ghost town—only a few die-hards remained.

The Steamboat *Charles E. Cessna*—Circa 1915

Pictured on Santa Rosa Plantation Company's stationery, the *Charles E. Cessna* was stated to have cost fifty thousand dollars. The steamboat carried folks that had recently arrived at Pensacola's train station to the new settlement between 1909 and 1918. Photo provided by the author.

Santa Rosa Assemblage—Circa 1916

Though the occasion for this gathering is not known, it must have been special as the Santa Rosa Plantation residents were dressed in their finest. Caroline Ziel is standing in the front row holding her baby Inez, with young daughter Carlotta standing close by. Courtesy, Norma Ziel Truelove.

We returned to our home, but it was stipulated in the agreement that my father would have four months before giving possession of their beautiful home. Lafayette told my father that he would assist him in building a new home on his, Lafayette's, land at the Horseshoe Bayou, which he did.

At this same time, brother Tilden moved his family to Portland and opened up a grocery store, living in the house across the road. There was no other store in Portland. Chandler, a first cousin, helped in the store. Tilden still owned the schooner *Evelyn* and made trips to Pensacola and brought back supplies for his store and other stores in the vicinity, such as those in Freeport and Whitfield. I made a model of Tilden's boat, the *Evelyn*, out of red cedar. It adorns the mantle in our living room, and when I cast my eyes upon it, it brings back the early years of my life on Choctawhatchee Bay.

**Model of Tilden's boat, the *Evelyn*
Courtesy, Anne and W. Homer Reddick, Jr.**

My father and mother lived at Horseshoe Bayou until Lafayette's family was grown up and all left home several years later. Lafayette moved to Daytona Beach, Florida, where most of his married children had moved. Father and Mother could not live alone, so they moved to Freeport across the Choctawhatchee Bay to live with my brother Tilden.

In 1952, forty-one years after we sold the home on Four Mile Point, my son Homer and I visited the old home, or rather the place where our home was. Some homes had been built on the Bay-front and we talked to one of the men who lived there. He showed us the pump and pipe that once supplied us with drinking water in our backyard. It was standing about 150 feet out in the Bay, which showed how the land had eroded since we lived there. There were some signs of the orange trees, as I found some sprouts in a broom straw lot that I figured could have been some of our orange tree sprouts.

PART II

Life as a Railroad Man

Chapter 16
Telegraph Operator

With the family home on Four Mile Peninsula sold, brother John and I decided that we would leave the Choctawhatchee Bay. Neither of us was employed at that time. I had been asked by my sister Jeannette and her husband, E. H. Jernigan, to come to Noma and live with them and help out in the store and post office. Both of us got passage on Tilden's schooner to Pensacola. John then took a train for New Orleans, where he attended a barber college for over a year and I went by train on to Noma.

After I worked in the store and attended school for a short time, I made up my mind to attend the Massey Business College in Montgomery. I talked this matter over with Jeannette and her husband and they thought it was a great idea. The problem was that I would have to get someone to work in my place at the store and post office. I contacted an old schoolmate of mine, Homer Johnson, who once lived in Point Washington. We were real close friends. I found out that he was in Bonifay, Florida, at that time and was not employed, so I asked him to come over to Noma and work in my place. He accepted and stayed with sister Jeannette. After I finished at Massey's, I returned to Noma and resumed my work in the store. Homer returned to Bonifay, where he received employment in the Hughes Mercantile Store.

Soon after I returned, I bought an interest in the E. H. Jernigan store at Noma and was made assistant postmaster. As the county of Holmes began to fill up with people, demands for better mail service were made. There was already a U.S. rural free delivery from Esto, a small town about three miles south of Noma. The post office inspector

Sister, Jeannette Reddick Jernigan

Jeannette Reddick Jernigan, holding baby Helen in her arms, stands in front of her Noma family home, on July 11, 1916, with her children, Valeta, Inita, Gail, and Glynn. Courtesy, Helen Jernigan Scivicque.

Brother-in-law, E. H. Jernigan

The Noma post office began service on August 20, 1902, about eight months after a post office was started in Esto, two miles away. Records show that E. H. Jernigan became postmaster December 19, 1908, and held the office until the local lumber mill closed down late in 1921. Courtesy, Helen Jernigan Scivicque.

came down and established an RFD route from Noma, which took off some of the Esto route and added it onto the Noma route, making some dissatisfied patrons.

Next there would be held a competitive examination in Noma to select a carrier for the route. There were only three of us that took the examination—Marion Turner, the sawmill foreman; Wiley C. Cameron; and myself. Mr. Turner, a Spanish-American War veteran, was automatically given fifty percent advantage in points in the examination and he, of course, was the highest. As foreman at the large sawmill Mr. Turner received a much better salary, so he declined the position as carrier. I was next in line, having made the higher rate over Mr. Cameron, and received the appointment.

I did not have any conveyance to carry the mail, but my brother-in-law, the postmaster, had a horse and buggy which he let me have until I could get a motorcycle. The roads over the twenty-seven-mile route were bad. Some of the dissatisfied patrons made it tough for me as an RFD carrier, but I withstood all the hardships for several months. A motorcycle salesman came along in town and wanted to sell me one of his Indian motorcycles and asked me to try it out. I did very well until the wheels got into the deep sand ruts of the road. It went out of control and threw me off—I landed about fifteen feet into a briar patch. I gave up the motorcycle.

So I continued to leave the post office with the horse and buggy about seven o'clock and when I returned it was about dark. Most of the time it was pouring down rain. It didn't take long to convince myself that this was not the job for me, so I notified the post office department that I was resigning. Mr. Wiley C. Cameron, next in line, was commissioned and, with a motorcycle, successfully carried the mail. I resumed my position in the store.

Brother John, while in New Orleans, had purchased a barber shop. He and Miss Ida Davis, whom I have mentioned during my associations with the Wesley family at Point Washington, became engaged. She was finishing A. B. Beeson's College in Hattiesburg, and they arranged to meet on a train that was stopping there. After having engaged a minister to be at the station when the train stopped, all got aboard the train. After the conductor caught on to what was happening,

Noma, Florida
A Town Created by the Railroad

THE PLANS FOR RAILROADS throughout Florida were put to a halt in the 1860s with the outbreak of the War between the States. It was another twenty years before building of the railways got back on track. The Louisville and Nashville Railroad completed the Pensacola to River Junction (Chattahoochee) track in 1883, bringing freight and passenger traffic through Northwest Florida.

About sixteen years after completion of the east/west Florida railroad line, the Louisville and Nashville undertook construction of another railroad through the lush pines of North Florida. The hundred miles of track, originating in Georgiana, Alabama, terminated in the town of Graceville in Holmes County. Completed on July 16, 1902, the route brought sawmill and turpentine industry to the towns of Esto and Noma and other small communities that sprang up along the route.

The *Florida Gazetteer* for 1911-12 credits Noma with a population of nine hundred. The dusty roads were lined with many businesses and public buildings: a high school (the first in Holmes County), a large lumber company, turpentine distilleries, three general stores, a newspaper office, a millinery, a meat market, a post office, a cotton gin, two hotels, several livery stables, and a barbershop. There were two druggists, a blacksmith, two notary publics, two physicians, a real estate salesman, and a justice of the peace. Town officials placed the population at fifteen-hundred in 1916 when the Alabama and Florida Lumber Company was operating at full capacity to meet demands created by World War I, then raging in Europe.

Noma remained a prosperous community for about twenty years until the region's old-growth pine forest was exhausted. Many people left town when the jobs disappeared, but the Louisville and Nashville Railroad continued operation through Noma until 1984.

he delayed the train until the minister performed the wedding ceremony.

Brother John and his bride went to New Orleans on their honeymoon, and he closed his shop and had all the equipment crated and shipped by railroad to Noma. It was several days before his barber shop arrived, and when it did, he rented a building across the street from our store. But he soon found out that the town was not large enough for two barber shops.

By this time I had been connected with my brother-in-law, E. H. Jernigan, for almost seven years. We decided to sell the store to Mr. W. P. DeShazo of Esto. My brother-in-law owned the other barber shop and when we sold the store, I received it in the settlement of my share, so John closed his shop and I let him operate mine. He was not there very long before Ida became ill and he had to take her to Montgomery and admit her into Dr. Blue's hospital. When she was able he returned her to Noma, but she was never well thereafter. Finally she died and was buried in the Noma cemetery with her newly born baby.

All the time that I was in the small town of Noma I enjoyed being with the young ladies that came there to teach school or music. I will not venture to say that I was a favorite among them, but I was accused of being the first to date a new one that came to town. Sometimes I would find myself in bad trouble by having more dates than I had time to fulfill, but I managed to wiggle out of that situation in some way. I remember when a young lady from Samson, Alabama, resigned her teaching position and another one was sent in her place. She also was from Samson—her name was Miss Lillian Anderson.

We were in the process of having a live vaudeville play at the high school auditorium. The play was *John Aulden and Priscilla* and I was to play the part of John Aulden. The girl that was to play the Priscilla part became ill and we had to find another. I was coming out of my sister's house when I met two ladies on the corner of the street who were going to the same prayer meeting at the Methodist Church as I was. The one I knew introduced me to her friend, the new music teacher, Miss Lillian Anderson. She was aware of the illness of the lady that had the Priscilla part. I asked her if she would take the part and she agreed.

By this time I had begun my long career with the railroad. I was working for Louisville and Nashville Railroad at McGee's Switch, a passing point for trains going north and south, for one week before being relieved by one of the three operators who had been in court in Montgomery. My next assignment was to relieve the agent/operator at Black, Alabama. He had gone to Montgomery to be admitted in the hospital and treated for some broken glass in his eyes and face. When he was opening the door to his office one night, someone threw a glass bottle, which hit the door near his face and shattered. I was in Black for several weeks before the agent returned and relieved me.

> ### Occupations Held by the Author during his Thirty-seven-Year Railroad Career
>
> The *telegraph operator* or *operator* used Morse code to transmit all messages sent by Western Union Telegraph Company, as well as to report the trains in and out from the station to the dispatcher.
>
> The *agent* was usually found in smaller stations where one person handled all the responsibilities of the office: telegraph operator, freight agent, and ticket accountant.
>
> The *rate clerk* or *clerk* would look up the freight tariffs, keeping up with all the changes and rules set by the Interstate Commerce Commission, and giving the information to the freight agent so the proper fee would be charged on all freight.
>
> The *freight agent* took the current rates from the rate clerk and made out the weigh bill. He also handled all the loading and unloading of freight.
>
> The *ticket accountant*, *accountant*, or *cashier* sold all the tickets to the passengers, keeping a stub and balancing his cash with the stubs at the end of the day.
>
> The *chief clerk* was the office foreman, responsible for all the work in the depot.

Life as a Railroad Man

While I was not out on relief assignment, I made Noma my headquarters and took up my duties of meeting the nine o'clock night train. At this particular time I was dating one of two sisters who lived with their father, their home being near the depot. The father thought I was a villain and was opposed to me dating his daughter. Miss Anderson was boarding in this home at the time, and her date this one night was Mr. Slater. Both he and I showed up to this home at the same time and the four of us played games until almost nine o'clock. I had to excuse myself for a short while to meet the train and handle the baggage. After the train was by and I had locked the office, I started back to be with my date and Slater and Miss Anderson as ten o'clock was the deadline for leaving. I met Slater on my way back to the house, and he told me that the old man ran him off. The father thought that it was Slater that left instead of me and used something to rap on the side of the wall next to the parlor, which was a signal for me to leave. I thought it was a good joke on Slater.

Soon after this occurrence I began dating Miss Anderson. The play came off with flying colors, and it was immediately rumored that this make-believe romance might be the beginning of the real thing by the participants, which turned out to be true as Miss Anderson became my wife.

I had a message from the chief dispatcher to fill the clerk position at Samson. He advised that this was a permanent position if I should want it, so I reported there the next day for work. I had been in Samson before and did not like the place, and leaving my girlfriend behind at Noma made me dislike Samson more than ever. I didn't have to work on Sundays so I'd take the train back to Noma to see my girlfriend and also confer with my good friend Mr. J. Lee Woodall, the Louisville and Nashville Railroad agent in Noma, about my contemplated change in position.

One day I was approached by Woodall and asked if I would be interested in a railroad career as a telegraph operator as the small station in Noma, as well as other stations, had to handle all the Western Union Telegraph Company's telegrams. We had talked this matter over and he told me that the railroad would pay me twenty dollars per month to study telegraphy and continue meeting the nine o'clock night train,

Some Early Railroad Routes of

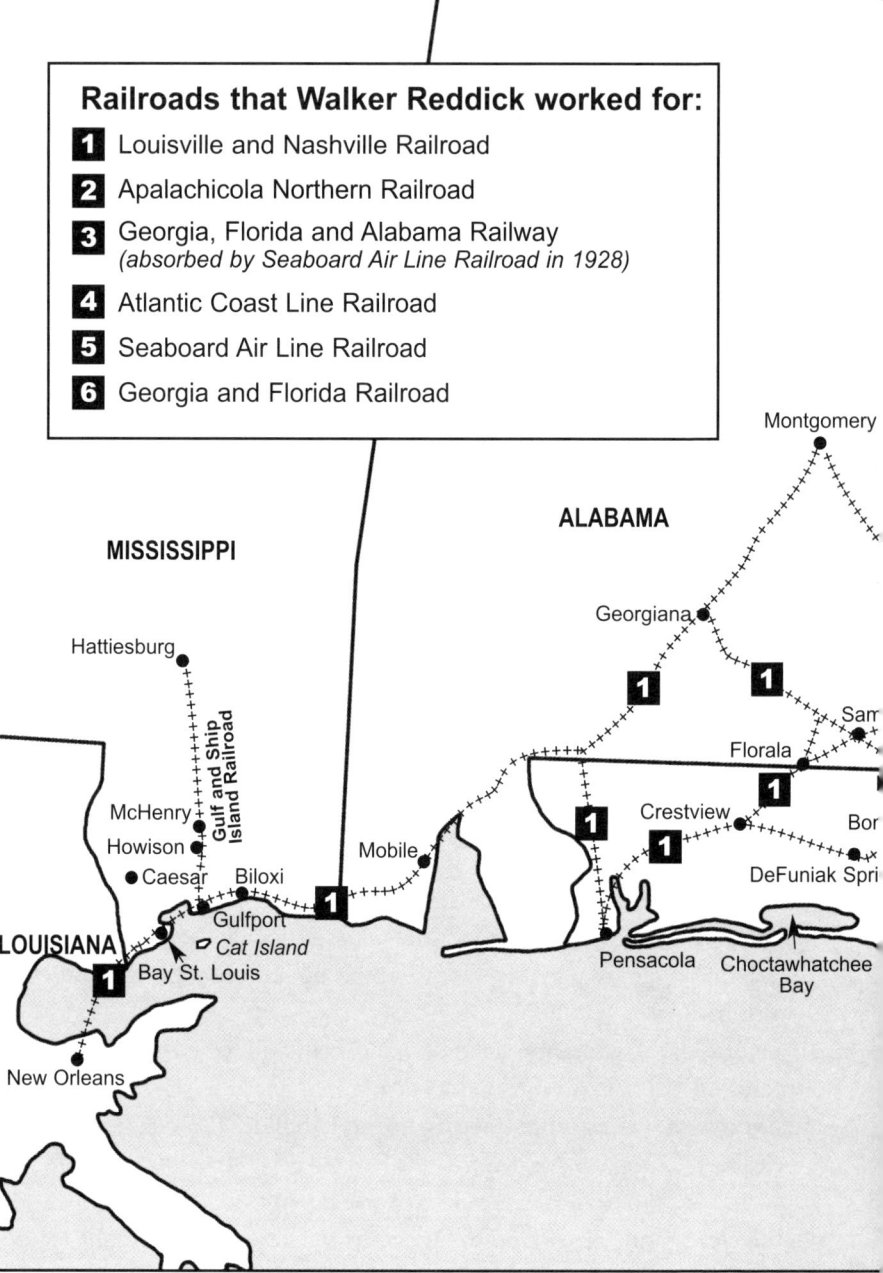

the Southeastern United States

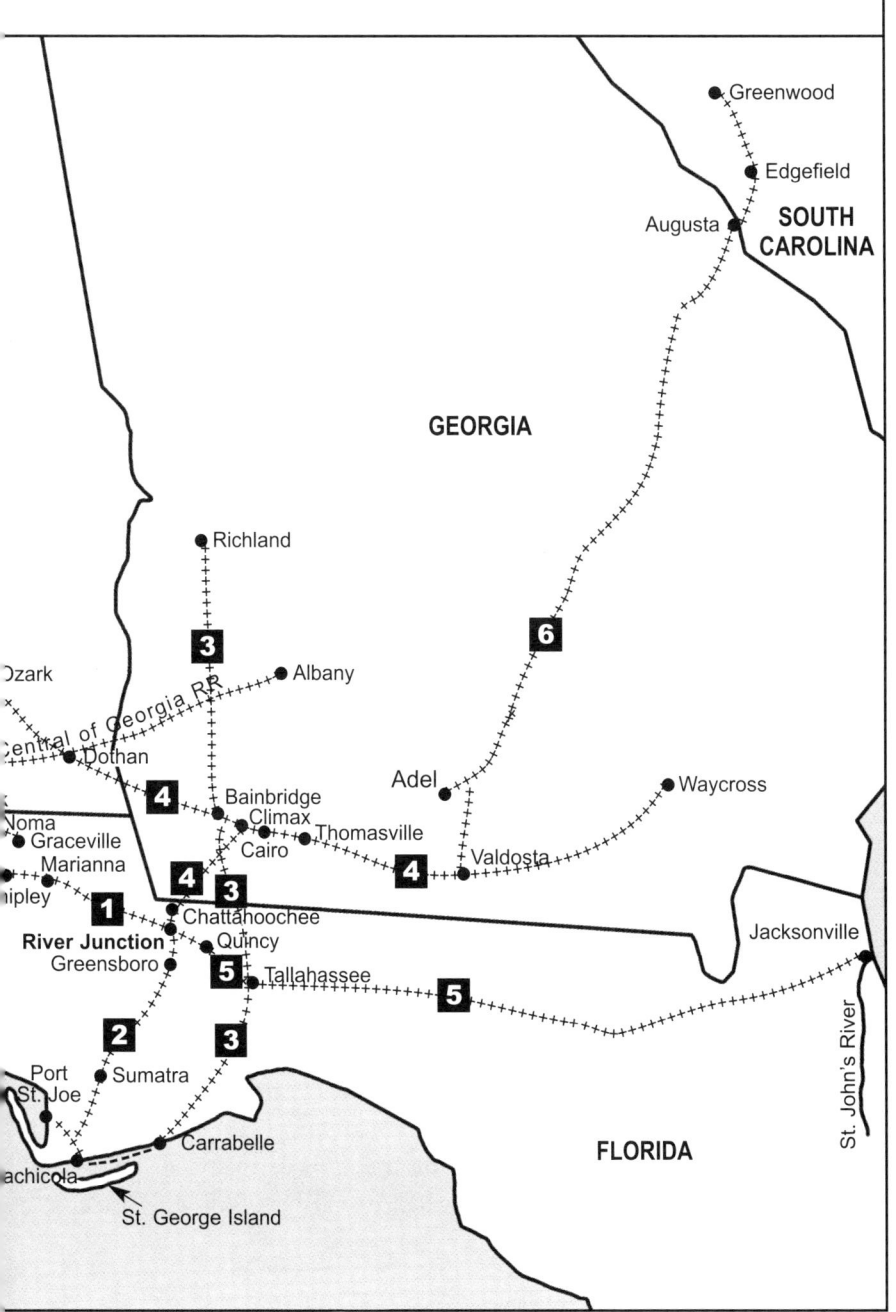

putting the baggage into the warehouse and locking it up. I agreed so Mr. Woodall and I strung some wire up into the warehouse that reached from one end to the other. He had some extra instruments and batteries that we set up and we were then ready for business. First I had to learn the alphabet—the Morse system. He would send to me and I would copy. I spent many hours practicing and it was not very long before I could report the trains in and out from the station to the dispatcher in Georgiana, Alabama.

I soon was proficient enough that Mr. Woodall could slip off and go hunting, and I would handle all of the office work, including handling all messages, telegrams, selling tickets, and freight rates from the many tariffs on file in the office. The procedure continued for several months until one day Mr. A. C. Avinger, the dispatcher, called me on the wires and told me to come to Georgiana and take the operator's examination. I was a little nervous about it but Mr. Woodall told me that he knew I would pass the examination. I had the advantage over some of the students just starting out because I knew how to do all of the office work as well as doing the telegraphing.

I went to Georgiana as requested and stood and passed the examination and was immediately sent to McGee's Switch. There were two other greenhorns also, and all three of us worked together day and night. One time we had several trains tied up there and a stack of train orders several inches thick. A tall man got off one of the trains and came in the telegraph office, sat down at the telegraph table, and began to get some of the trains out. He didn't introduce himself until after he cleared out all the trains, and then he told us that he was Frank Young, the chief dispatcher from the Montgomery office. Had we known that it was him we would have been more nervous and excited.

I confided in my good friend Woodall and he agreed that I might be happier working at some point closer to my old home on the coast. However, he also regretted my decision to leave the Louisville and Nashville Railroad. He remembered how much help I had been to him while I was a student in his office. At this time I made an application by wire with the Apalachicola Northern Railroad at Port St. Joe, Florida, for employment.

School was drawing to a close in Noma and my girlfriend would be returning to her home in Samson soon. She and I were invited by the couple she was boarding with to attend the Confederate Veterans Reunion in Jacksonville, Florida, with them. It was to be held in just a short time and we accepted their invitation. I had already resigned by letter to the Louisville and Nashville Railroad Company. My cousin E. L. "Dick" Reddick, whose headquarters were in Jacksonville, was contacted and told of our plans to attend the reunion and asked to make hotel reservations for our party. He met us at the train and escorted us to the Westmoreland Hotel, where we remained for three days. One of the days was spent on board a large excursion boat, which took us down St. John's River. We enjoyed the excursion very much. Afterwards we returned to Chipley where a car was waiting to take us back to Noma. Miss Anderson then returned to her home in Samson for the summer.

Chapter 17
Wedding Bells

I received a telegram from Mr. D. Sullivan, the superintendent of the Apalachicola Northern Railroad at Port St. Joe, to report to Apalachicola the following Monday morning to work the first trick [shift] telegraph operator's job. Mr. Ross Henderson, the agent, took me around to Mrs. Kinsey's boarding house where I was given a room and meals. I was not on this job very long before they had a vacancy at Sumatra, Florida, as agent/operator, which suited me as I had much training in freight and express rates and selling tickets. My salary at that time was fifty dollars per month plus express commissions, which was, indeed, more than the Apalachicola job paid. I boarded with Mrs. Spence, who was a widow with two daughters, one of them being the wife of Bob Ferrell, whom I relieved as agent there. During my stay at Sumatra I was in close touch with my girlfriend. Miss Anderson had visited her sister, Mrs. J. C. Helms, and in the fall taught music in the Compass Lake, Florida, schools until April 1916, when she returned home to Samson, at which time we became engaged.

My memory takes me back to a short time before my brother-in-law, E. H. Jernigan, and I sold the mercantile business in Noma. I usually went to the store early in the morning and opened up the post office and made ready for the RFD carrier to get his mail to make delivery on his route. There was a lobby to the post office from the outside so patrons could get their mail after the store had been closed. Occasionally someone would leave his box unlocked and anyone could reach in through the box and pick up anything that might be left on the table just inside of the office. The money drawer, where we kept the stamp money, could also be easily reached from one of the mail boxes nearest to the cash drawer.

While I was in the store early one morning I saw a small Negro boy reaching through one of the boxes that had been left unlocked, opening the drawer, and taking all the cash out. Before he could get out of the lobby I caught him and called the police. He was locked up, and the following day I was summoned to appear before the U.S. commissioner in Marianna, Florida, as a witness at the commitment hearing. The commissioner bound the boy over to the U.S. Federal Court in Pensacola. The commissioner told me that I would receive another summons to appear in Federal Court when it convened in Pensacola. The court convened the last of April 1916 and I notified the superintendent of the Apalachicola Northern Railroad for leave to appear. I immediately notified my girlfriend at Compass Lake of my plans—after the case had been disposed of, I would proceed to Samson and we would get married and return to the general office in Port St. Joe, where I was temporarily working in the freight office until the ticket accountant's job came open.

I arrived in Samson on May 4, 1916, and my bride-to-be was waiting. We excitedly made plans for our wedding the following day—my twenty-seventh birthday. That night I took the train for Noma, only about forty miles from Samson, to spend the night at my sister Jeannette's, arriving at nine o'clock. Early the next morning I took the train to Geneva on my way back to Samson. I had to stop in Geneva, the county seat, to secure the wedding license. The courthouse didn't open up until nine A.M. and for this time of year it was cold. I was wearing a white Palm Beach suit and was about to freeze before the lady clerk of the court opened up the office. But when she did I asked her to issue me a marriage license. She looked at me and asked who the bride was to be. I told her Miss Lillian Anderson of Samson. She said she knew her very well and that I was getting an adorable girl. I also purchased my wedding suit in Geneva. As there was no train to take me back to Samson, I had to get a taxi—the distance was fourteen miles—and the minister was to be at Miss Anderson's home at ten o'clock.

Future wife, Lillian Lea Anderson

"I arrived in Samson on May 4, 1916, and my bride-to-be was waiting. We excitedly made plans for our wedding the following day—my twenty-seventh birthday." Courtesy, Anne and W. Homer Reddick, Jr.

On arriving in Samson I engaged a room at the hotel and took a bath, donned my wedding clothes, and proceeded to her home. I was late and the minister, Brother Simms, had another engagement and was anxious to get the ceremony over with. After the ceremony, lunch was prepared for us and then we boarded the Central of Georgia train for Florala where we spent the night before proceeding on to Port St. Joe.

When we arrived at River Junction, Florida, on the Louisville and Nashville line, the large hotel near the depot was on fire and the depot was in danger of burning also. After a three-hour wait, our Apalachicola Northern train left for Apalachicola and on to Port St. Joe. As the locomotive chucked and churned on down the rickety and rocky road, the two of us fought the cinders flowing into the coach through the unscreened windows. Apalachicola was a stop-over station for refueling and taking on a supply of water for the rest of the trip. When the train stopped in Apalachicola, a committee came aboard the train to greet and congratulate and offer felicitations, showering us with an abundance of rice, which was not only all over us, but all over the coach we occupied. I don't know how these folks knew that we were bride and groom unless the operator in River Junction let the cat out when he copied the pass for my wife before we left River Junction. It was getting late at night when we arrived at Port St. Joe and Mr. J. P. Linton, the freight agent, met us and took us to his home to spend the night.

The railroad, during the summer months, ran an excursion into Port St. Joe and sometimes it ran a second section of the train to bring all the passengers to the small seaport town. There was a large hotel down on the waterfront with a wide dock extending far out into the St. Joseph Bay. One day I thought I would take my wife down on the dock where many skiff boats were available and take her out into the Bay for a ride into the waters, which she had not been used to.

I had my bride settled into the front of the skiff and untied the rope from the dock. While I went aft to use the oar to guide the boat out into the Bay, I looked around to see if she was seated and saw her holding onto the dock. The boat continued going out away from the dock, and she plunged flat out and face down into the water. I immediately jumped into the water and rescued her and lifted her back into the boat. There were hundreds of people at the hotel who had a

Bustling Crowd at Port St. Joe Depot—Circa 1915

Each day at noon the Apalachicola Northern train arrived at the Port St. Joe depot loaded with tourists ready to enjoy the white sand beaches and good fishing. Courtesy, Florida State Archives.

St. Joe Dock, Port St. Joe—Circa 1917

The three loading tracks on the St. Joe Dock extended a half-mile into the Bay, allowing convenient transfer of freight and passengers between trains and ships. The steamer *Farnham* is tied up next to the dock, loaded with crates containing aircraft parts bound for France during World War I. Courtesy, Billy Howell collection.

clear view of what went on. Both of us were soaking wet and had to walk through a laughing crowd on the dock and through the hotel. She never rode with me in a boat again, as I remember. We were soon over all this humiliation and didn't let it keep us away from the water—we'd used a flashlight to catch crabs with a sharp spear. I remember my wife jumping into the air one night when a crab bit her on one of her toes.

There was a narrow sand peninsula separating the Gulf of Mexico from the St. Joseph Bay. No one inhabited this peninsula because there was no vegetation growing there. Also, it was vulnerable to high winds and storms. When a squall came up and the winds caused high seas, it was not safe for small boats to be caught out in the Bay. But that didn't stop people from crossing the Bay and fishing for speckle-back crabs, which were plentiful over there. There was a camp shed built on the Bay-side of the peninsula equipped with tables and large wash pots to boil crabs in.

Mr. Linton owned a small motor boat and asked me to go with him over to the sand peninsula one day to catch some crabs. I accepted his invitation. The boat didn't have any life preservers aboard, no oars or paddles of any kind. When we arrived about halfway across the Bay, one of those squalls came up and the seas began to rise high. Our motor failed us, and there we were, helpless and in grave danger of the boat floundering. It was too far from either side of the Bay for us to swim. The boat began to take water, and we had only a small coffee can to bail it out.

Luck was with us though. The winds subsided and the motor finally started, and we made it safely to the peninsula. We soon had all the crabs we wanted and boiled them in one of the pots. We had some ketchup and crackers and really did enjoy ourselves. However, that was my last trip across the Bay on Mr. Linton's small boat.

The St. Joseph Bay was very deep, allowing access for large ships to come in and dock at the half-mile-long dock. The railroad tracks that ran out on the dock were owned by the Apalachicola Northern Railroad Company, but that part of the line was called the St. Joe Dock Company. When ships came into the dock to take on a cargo of lumber, the railroad would switch the cars that were loaded with lumber to the ship's side and make a separate billing, which the ship would

The Port Inn, Port St. Joe—Circa 1915

The Port Inn, with its wide dock extending far out into the St. Joseph Bay, was built in 1912 by the Apalachicola Northern Railroad to provide overnight lodging for the tourists seeking a holiday at the beach. "One day I thought I would take my wife…out into the Bay for a ride into the waters.… I had my bride settled into the front of the skiff and untied the rope from the dock. While I went aft to use the oar to guide the boat out into the Bay, I looked around … and saw her holding onto the dock.… She plunged flat out and face down into the water. I immediately jumped into the water and rescued her and lifted her back into the boat.… Both of us were soaking wet and had to walk through a laughing crowd on the dock and through the hotel." Courtesy, Billy Howell Collection.

have to pay, as well as the freight charge. This dock was an ideal place to fish. Mr. Linton and I often fished out there and I remember we caught a large stingray and landed him on the dock. He must have weighed seventy-five pounds.

A bad accident happened on the dock after we had moved from Port St. Joe. Mr. D. Sullivan, the railroad superintendent, was walking out on the dock while cars of lumber were being switched, and the standards holding the lumber on one car broke. All the lumber fell on Mr. Sullivan, killing him instantly.

Apalachicola Northern Railroad

RIVER JUNCTION, southeast of Chattahoochee, Florida, was the juncture of the Atlantic Coast Line, Seaboard, and Louisville and Nashville Railroads, connecting north Florida with Atlanta and other southeastern cities. With the Panama Canal under construction, a rail line was needed to link with the Gulf of Mexico so shipments could be loaded on ocean-going vessels and marketed worldwide. So in 1907, two years after the start of construction, the Apalachicola Northern Railroad was completed, linking River Junction with Apalachicola Bay.

But before the line was finished it was realized that the shallow Apalachicola Bay wouldn't be able to handle large ships. The thirty-five- foot-deep St. Joseph Bay, twenty miles to the west, was the answer to the problem. Completed in 1910, the branch connecting the tracks above Apalachicola to Port St. Joe successfully diverted the bulk of passenger and freight trains from Apalachicola. Within eight years Port St. Joe grew to be an industrial center and port.

The rail line shipped oysters, shrimp, and canned fish from these seaport villages, along with cuttings of the old-growth forest that surrounded the tracks. It is estimated that local lumber yielded four to five billion board-feet of yellow pine, harvested and transported by rail and ship, wiping the countryside barren within twenty years.

The Steamboat *Crescent City*—Circa 1910

The Georgia, Florida and Alabama Railroad completed the 183 miles of track from Richland, Georgia, to the coastal town of Carrabelle, Florida, in 1908. The company's side-paddle steamer, the *Crescent City*, provided connecting service between the trains at Carrabelle and the town of Apalachicola. Courtesy, Florida State Archives.

Life as a Railroad Man

It was only a short time before Mr. Drake, the accountant in Apalachicola, put in his resignation. After Mr. Drake left office, I took over his assignment and worked a few weeks, before the joint freight agent at River Junction was shot and killed. It was the Apalachicola Northern Railroad time to fill the joint agency with an agent, so the general manager appointed Mr. Linton, their freight agent at Port St. Joe, to fill the position. They asked me to fill Mr. Linton's freight agency job for a few days, until they could get the place filled permanently, and I agreed.

The freight agent of the Georgia, Florida and Alabama Railway at Apalachicola, Mr. Dewitt Marks, approached me and informed me that he was leaving the railroad to help his father, Mr. H. D. Marks, operate his wholesale grocery business, which was in the same building as the railroad office was. In fact, Mr. Marks owned the building. The salary was more attractive than the Apalachicola Northern Railroad was paying me, so I resigned and accepted the Georgia, Florida and Alabama agency at Apalachicola. The trains of this railway came into the terminal at Carrabelle, Florida, and the company's side-paddle steamer provided connecting service with Apalachicola. This steamship, the *Crescent City*, handled freight and passengers.

A short time after I took over the office, I secured a pass for my wife to visit with her father in Samson. She was still afraid of the water after the incident in Port St. Joe when she fell into the water off of the dock, but the good captain on the *Crescent City* assured her that it would be perfectly safe for her passage on the steamboat. Captain Wing told me on his return to Apalachicola that he helped her to the train in Carrabelle and she was on her way. She was traveling alone and had to change to the Central of Georgia Railroad in Georgia, but made the trip safely to her father's home.

I will mention here that steamboats, including the *Crescent City*, discharged and took on freight from the canning factories operating on either side of my office on the docks. These factories mostly canned oysters and shrimp which were cooked in large retorts, put into cans, and packed in boxes for shipment all over the United States. The oysters were also shelled by hand in the factories and put into half-gallon cans or barrels, packed in ice, and shipped out by express to all points. By my solicitation and regular visits to the shipper's office, I received a good share of the outbound and inbound freight for the Georgia, Florida and Alabama Railroad in Apalachicola. My wife and I had all the shrimp and oysters that we needed.

The only necessity that we did not like and could not get used to was the sulfur water. We were fortunate in having lived in a small city that had the distinction of having such an inventive man as Dr. John Gorrie to discover ice. His monument was plainly visible from our apartment in the Hickey home, standing in a prominent place in the city.

Another interesting character in Apalachicola was Mr. William Lee Popham, a poet, who was living over on St. George Island along with other families. Mr. Popham was leasing oyster beds. I do not recall exactly his business, but I usually went over there with DeWitt Marks to deliver groceries to them on a motor boat.

The Gorrie Monument, Apalachicola

STILL STANDING SINCE 1899 in its prominent location behind the Trinity Episcopal Church in Apalachicola, the monument to honor Dr. John Gorrie is a proud symbol to the people of Apalachicola. But why was it erected by the Southern Ice Exchange?

In 1841 yellow fever was attacking the Gulf coast of Florida, nearly wiping out many coastal communities. The dreaded onset of symptoms of headache, backache, rapidly rising fever, and nausea lasted for a couple of days. At this point the patient either recovered—to be forever immune—or began to turn yellow from jaundice, the liver cells having been destroyed. Vomiting mouthfuls of dark blood and lapsing into a coma, the patient died within a day. Home after home would sadly display a yellow flag to alert others to keep away.

Dr. John Gorrie, a resident of Apalachicola since 1833, noticed that many yellow fever patients recovered with the changing seasons and became convinced that cold was the remedy, providing a method of combating fevers. He set to work to invent a machine to make ice to be used to lower the temperature in the hospital rooms. Dr. Gorrie's yellow-fever patients kept in sealed, ice-cooled rooms were reported to make faster recoveries. Fifty years later it was proven that yellow fever was transmitted by the bite of a mosquito.

Dr. Gorrie was granted the first U.S. patent for mechanical refrigeration in 1851. His invention led him to be recognized as the father of modern-day manufacturing of ice, refrigeration, and air conditioning, an invention we can all be thankful for. The State of Florida honored Dr. Gorrie in 1911 by including his statue in the Statuary Hall in Washington, D.C. Photo by the editor.

William Lee Popham
Author, Poet, and Traveler

THIRTY-ONE-YEAR-OLD William Lee Popham arrived in Apalachicola in January 1917, when he preached at the local Methodist church, even though he was a Baptist preacher. An evangelist since the age of seventeen, Mr. Popham was quite the Renaissance man. He was a prolific writer of essays, prose, and love stories, having published eight books of poetry, essays, sermons, and fiction in 1910 alone. Popham lectured on the Chautauqua circuit from 1907 to 1912 and was an instant success. His audience, no matter if it was one person on the street or thousands in an auditorium, was held spell-bound. According to William Rogers' book, *Outposts on the Gulf*, Mr. Popham was described as "verbose," "a downright talker," "gentle in language and never cursing," and "completely convincing."

This industrious man bought St. George Island across the Apalachicola Bay in 1918 from George W. Saxon, selling price $30,000, using the copyrights to all of his books as security, and leased the water bottoms in the Apalachicola Bay for oyster production.

This is where his way with words came in handy. Mr. Popham began promoting St. George Island, selling warranty deeds to lots fifty-foot by one-hundred-foot for twelve hundred dollars plus interest, payable at ten dollars per month for twenty years. Along with the property, the purchaser would share in the profits from the sale of the oyster beds with the other investors in the Oyster Growers' Co-Operative Association. It is thought he received thousands of dollars a day from monthly payments.

Popham published this pamphlet promoting St. George Island. Courtesy, Florida State Archives.

Chapter 18
Surviving the 1918 Influenza Epidemic

World War I was declared by this country on April 2, 1917, and I was called up for examination and probable draft into the service. But the railroads needed men badly as they were carrying a heavy load, passenger troop movements, and also war materiel. Our superintendent, Mr. Jim Bowdoin, gave the government a list of employees that he urgently needed to operate the railroads, and I was on that list and exempt from serving in the military service.

I worked with the Georgia, Florida and Alabama Railway for some time when the Apalachicola Northern Railroad came to me and offered me a sizable increase in salary to take the Greensboro, Florida, agency, which I did. While we lived in Greensboro, our first child was born on September 4, 1917, a sweet little girl. We asked each of our fathers to name her. My father said name her Lee and my wife's father said name her Lillian, so we put the two names together and named her Lillian Lee. Our next move was to Port St. Joe where I worked as the ticket accountant. Mr. Linton, who was now at River Junction, called me on the wires one day and wanted me to go to River Junction and take the cashier's job for all four of the railroads there.

We moved from Port St. Joe to River Junction about November 1, 1917. Our little daughter, Lillian Lee, was then about two months old. The joint cashier's job was shaping up for me to take over, but the superintendent of the Atlantic Coast Line was short of a man at Bainbridge, Georgia, and asked me to go over there and fill the place until the cashier's job opened up for me. He said it would be only a few days. I agreed to this, although I was sick, and went on over to

World War I Soldiers—Circa 1918

The railroads of the East Coast and port towns were filled with troops and military supplies during World War I. Courtesy, Florida State Archives.

Life as a Railroad Man

Bainbridge, leaving my wife and child at River Junction until I returned. I arrived in Bainbridge and reported to Mr. D. G. McLeland, the freight agent.

But the following day I went to see Dr. Chason, and after examination, he said I had pneumonia and should get a room at the hotel and go to bed. He came to see me the next morning and said that I should be in the hospital. The doctor, with the aid of the janitor at the hotel, took me downstairs and put me in his car. He carried me to the Riverside Hospital, which he owned. They found my pass in my clothing and got my address at River Junction. The folks at the hospital called my wife, the agent there, and the chief clerk, Mr. C. L. Moore. They brought my wife and baby over to the hospital at Bainbridge. My wife secured room and board at Mrs. Hill's rooming house across the street from the hospital and visited me several times each day for about three weeks. Her father, Mr. M. F. Anderson, also came over to be with my wife and baby for a few days, after which he returned to Samson.

By the time I was able to leave the hospital, I did not report for work at the freight office at Bainbridge, as the cashier's job at River Junction was ready for me. After recuperating and gaining my strength, I took over the joint cashier's position, which included the Apalachicola Northern Railroad, Seaboard Railroad, Louisville and Nashville Railroad, and the Atlantic Coast Line Railroad. I sold tickets and kept all cash accounts for all four of the lines.

This was a seven day a week job and my hours were eight to five, with one hour for lunch. There were twenty-four employees upstairs and four downstairs, not including the yard employees, who had offices in the roundhouse on the yard. Trains, both freight and passenger, came all times during the day and night. While I was not on duty during the night, the telegraph operators had to sell tickets for all lines and I had to check them up each morning and balance all four cash books each day.

I was about to forget to mention about the equipment we had in the office when I started to work at River Junction. My desk was a long one, and I had six or seven small brass lamps with spouts and rounded wicks that used slow-burning oil. When lighted, the lamps created a dense fog of black smoke that almost suffocated me. The light that

River Junction Depot and Yard—Circa 1920

River Junction Depot, now incorporated into the town of Chattahoochee, was the junction of four railroads: Atlantic Coast Line Railroad, Seaboard Air Line Railroad, Louisville and Nashville Railroad, and Apalachicola Northern Railroad. This allowed the southern towns and larger cities up north to be linked by rail. Many of the twenty-eight employees working in the office during the author's tenure performed their job for all four railroads, therefore their occupation would be "joint" telegraph operator, "joint" rate clerk, etc. Courtesy, Billy Howell Collection.

these small lamps gave out was so dim that it took a person with real good eyesight to see his work. There were many desks in the office and the janitor had to start in early afternoon gathering the lamps up and taking them to a separate room to refill them with the slow-burning oil and to trim the wicks and dry the oil off the outside. Sometimes they would leak, and when you lifted one of them off the desk it would cause an oil ring to be left on the desk. Electricity had not been heard of at that time, but if it had, it probably was cheaper to use the oil burners.

I will undertake to name some of the employees that worked in the office while I was there—J. P. Linton, agent; Charlie L. Moore, chief clerk; Mrs. Eva Herring; Mr. Dodge Shepard; Tip Spear; Ernest Eage (later was appointed general manager of the Birmingham Southern Railroad operating from Chipley to West Bay, Florida); Ralph McPhaul; Mr. Cheek, a Jew from Atlanta; Addie Shelfer; T. P. Harvard; W. N. Lemon; W. A. Runkle; Roy Colquit; and a waybill transfer clerk that chewed tobacco—I do not remember his name. Also Inita Jernigan, my niece from Quincy; Jim, the janitor; Jay Sammons; Joe Baggette; John Roberta; and Jimmy Peacock, the express clerk.

We were living in River Junction just a short time before our baby daughter got whooping cough. After our family doctor did all he could for her and she was getting worse, we asked him if he had any suggestions as to what we should do. He said that there was a good baby doctor in Montgomery and advised we take her to him. I made arrangements to be relieved at the office, and our doctor contacted Dr. Dawson in Montgomery. Dr. Dawson told him to bring the baby to him as quickly as we could get there. My wife and I immediately left with Lillian Lee for Montgomery, and on arrival, we rushed her to the doctor's office.

He examined her and gave us a prescription and told us to find lodging as close to his office as possible. With the first dose of the medicine, she turned almost black and would lose her breath when she coughed. We took her back to the doctor the following day, and he told us that he'd like to see her once a day for about three weeks. He also told us that he'd have her on cow's milk in a little while, but fed her Dime Brand milk for a short time. Before we took her to Dr. Dawson,

Walker H. Reddick, Sr. and Lillian Lee
Circa 1919

Courtesy, Anne and W. Homer Reddick, Jr.

Life as a Railroad Man

she could not retain Nestlé's baby formula and was almost dwindled away. I had to return to my job, but I left my wife and baby in Montgomery until it was safe for Lillian Lee to leave the doctor, after which time they returned home. The doctor was right, our baby was soon put on cow's milk and continued to get over the whooping cough as her health improved. Our baby was about eleven months old at this time.

At the beginning of World War I, brother Tilden sold his mercantile business and moved to Pensacola, where he worked at the shipyards building ships that were used for transporting soldiers to the war zone in Great Britain and France. After the war he bought a home in Freeport and reared his family. His sons were Coston L. Reddick, Sheldon Reddick, and Stelzie Reddick. All of the family have passed on except Coston, who lives in Jacksonville at this time [Coston died on January 21, 1981]. The others are buried in the same lot where my father and mother are buried in the Hatcher Cemetery, four miles west of Freeport.

My father heard about the Old Soldiers' Home in Jacksonville and decided that it might be best that he and my mother go live there for a while. I obtained leave from my job and took them to the home, which was some distance from the city up the St. John's River. When we arrived there, they were given a three-room villa on the grounds of the home. This was a beautiful place with many kinds of shade trees, and the old comrades of the Confederacy were seen in groups about the grounds exchanging stories about the Civil War.

Although my father thought it was a wonderful place, he soon began to get restless. I had to get off again from my work and bring them to Quincy, where sister Jeannette and her family lived, eighteen miles from my home in River Junction. I borrowed a horse and wagon to take their belongings to the express office in Jacksonville, on the opposite side of the city. I drove that horse and wagon through all of the busy streets there and back, but I made it safely. The Old Soldiers' Home's bus carried us to the Seaboard train that took us back to Quincy.

We were living in River Junction when Spanish Influenza first appeared in this country. In the office where I was working, twenty of

The Confederate Soldiers' and Sailors' Home—Circa 1897

Opening on April 6, 1893, on Talleyrand Avenue in Jacksonville, the Old Soldiers' Home sheltered Confederate veterans for forty-six years. The Florida chapters of the United Daughters of the Confederacy held balls and fairs to outfit the Home with bed and table linens, towels, coffee pots, and pitchers with wash basins. They furnished the men who had worn the gray with tobacco, fresh fruit and vegetables, sausage and hams, homemade bread and preserves. "[The Old Soldiers' Home] was a beautiful place with many kinds of shade trees, and the old comrades of the Confederacy were seen in groups about the grounds exchanging stories about the Civil War." Courtesy, Florida State Archives.

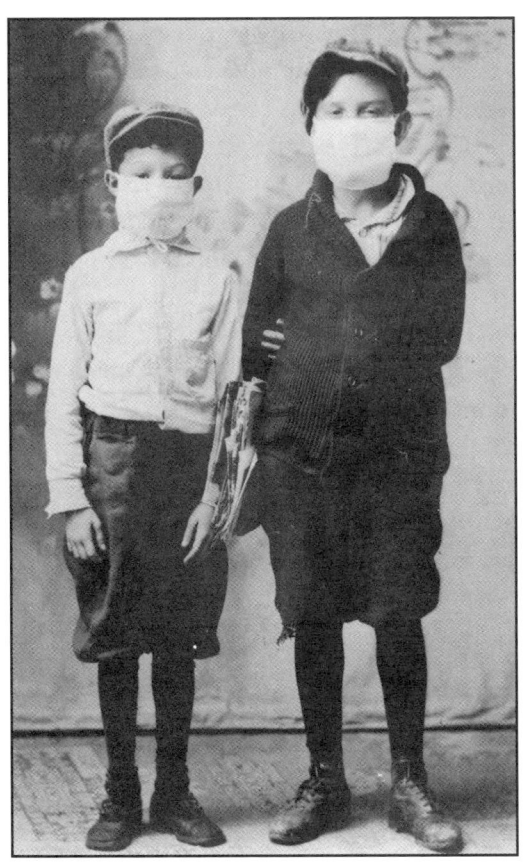

The Deadly Influenza Epidemic of 1918

Two Florida boys, readying themselves for school, don masks to protect them from the 1918 influenza epidemic. Five hundred and fifty thousand people died in the United States during this outbreak. Courtesy, Florida State Archives.

the twenty-four people upstairs and two of the four downstairs were out sick, caring for the sick, or helping to bury the dead. I happened to be one of the four upstairs who didn't have influenza. Neither did any of my family catch it. But as I was exposed to it day and night, I kept a ball of asafetida [a root credited with warding off the croup or whooping cough, with an odor stronger than an onion and a bitter and acrid taste] tied by a string about my neck and a ball of it in my mouth all the time. I attribute not having the influenza to that, and my family stayed close indoors at our home.

There were hardly enough employees left in the office to operate the trains, and people were crowding the trains, going everywhere trying to escape the influenza. The platform and all of the baggage and express dollies (high-bodied trucks) were filled with bodies of those who had died in the Florida State Hospital and were being shipped out by train to their respective homes for burial. These were scary times. No one seemed to know how to treat this influenza, even the doctors.

It was November 1918 when we received over the wires that Germany had surrendered and the war was over. The many steam locomotives in the railroad yard all gave several minutes of blasts of their whistles, and jubilance was in the air. After the influenza had subsided and the world had begun to get back to normal, the railroad employees that were out sick began returning to their respective jobs. There were great signs of thankfulness among all the occupants of the office.

About this time, August 20, 1919, another daughter was born, Marion Elizabeth. My mother was with us on that occasion and stayed with us a short time, after which she returned to sister Jeannette's at Quincy to be with my father. She was taken ill soon thereafter and was ailing for some time.

After I had been with the joint railroads for two years in the cashier's position, I was promoted to assistant chief clerk and joint rate clerk. My job was to fill the chief clerk's job when he was absent and to look up rates in the freight tariffs, file current supplements to these tariffs, and apply and figure proper rates to the freight bills, inter-line and local. The job was tough, but the pay was considered good.

Life as a Railroad Man

The bad part was that I was still working seven days per week without time off on Sunday for church services in the morning. But the First Baptist Church held a revival. The visiting minister was Reverend Hill from Birmingham, and the pastor was Reverend Frank Grant from Jacksonville. I was a member of the Methodist church, but my wife and children were Baptist. I joined the Baptist church during the revival and so did Joe Baggett, another one of the operators in my office. Both of us were baptized by the Reverend Grant in Huff's pool near Quincy.

We had purchased a home between River Junction and Chattahoochee and in this home on March 26, 1922, a son was born and named Walker Homer Reddick. This made three sweet children in our family.

By this time we had lived in River Junction about five years, and lots of "water had passed over the dam." Masters and Mullins Construction Company had finished building a new bridge over the Apalachicola River replacing an old wooden one. The new bridge was dedicated when finished—its opening well advertised. People were told to bring a full picnic basket and dinner would be served on the ground. Prominent speakers from Tallahassee were there to speak at the ribbon cutting. It rained all day and the slick lime and clay soil was plenty evident. There were not many automobiles in those days—had there been, everything would have been in a worse mess than it was. When cars did begin to appear in great numbers, it was found that the new bridge was not adequate to take care of the traffic, as it was too narrow and cars could hardly pass on the bridge.

The company that built the bridge discovered that the Apalachicola River bottom contained unlimited quantities of gravel and clean sand, and they capitalized on dredging this sand and gravel. The railroads furnished them with gondola cars and shipped several cars each day to building contractors all over the South.

Since that time, there has been a very wide rainbow bridge built to replace the Masters and Mullins bridge. This new bridge is high enough for large seagoing vessels to pass under. Also there has been built just north of the bridge, a dam with a dike to float ships through into the Seminole Lake, which was formed when the dam was constructed. The Chattahoochee and Flint Rivers come together and fill Lake Seminole

Victory Bridge, Near Chattahoochee—1922

River Junction and Chattahoochee townspeople gathered on the Apalachicola River bank for the dedication of the Victory Bridge on June 20, 1922. The first steamboat through the drawbridge was the *Callahan*, passing through the span twenty minutes after the dedication. Courtesy, Florida State Archives.

"When cars did begin to appear in great numbers, it was found that the new bridge was not adequate to take care of the traffic, as it was too narrow and cars could hardly pass on the bridge." Courtesy, Florida State Archives.

with water, making it a fisherman's paradise. This also made Bainbridge a seaport city, where large barges now arrive after plying the Flint River.

My father and mother were in very bad health while staying with my sister Jeannette. Brother John and I were sleeping in a room next to Mother's when she woke, sat up in the bed, and told sister Jeannette that the time was near and asked her to waken John and me. We went to her bedside, and she told us that she was leaving us, said goodbye, and instructed Jeannette to give me her Bible. I have it now and shall always revere it to the utmost. She died January 11, 1924, at the age of sixty-nine.

This Holy Bible was first owned by Ida Davis Redx Reddick. John H. Reddick's first wife. Itwas used used by her while she studying Bible in Beesons College in Meridian Mississippi. Before her passing, she gave the Bible to my Mother, Mrs. Elizabeth McCormick Reddick, who, at her death gave it to me, Walker H. Reddick Sr. New backs were replaced by Walker H. Reddick Sr. May 29th. 1978

Ida Davis bought the Bible about the turn of the century 1900.

At my passing I bequeath this Bible to my son W. Homer Reddick.

Walker H. Reddick Sr.

This the twenty nineth day of May AD 1978

Father took ill soon after my mother's death. He had been blind now for twelve years and needed constant care. Sister Jeannette was not physically able to continue to take care of him. Neither were we, having the two babies. I conferred with our family doctor, B. F. Barnes at River Junction, who was already familiar with our situation, and he advised that we admit him to the Florida State Hospital in Chattahoochee, not as an inmate, but as a patient. We took his advice, and as Dr. Barnes was on the staff, he suggested that he make all the arrangements for my father to be admitted. Father passed away June 28, 1924, five months after Mother's death, and was interred beside my mother in Hatcher Cemetery.

The History of Florida State Hospital

IT WAS 1856, eleven years after receiving statehood, when Florida enacted the first law for the mentally ill. This act enabled the "lunatics" to be removed from jails and housed in asylums—but not in Florida as there were no facilities.

Things changed when the State of Florida received an old arsenal from the Federal government. Fort Jackson, consisting of officers' quarters, barracks, magazines, a business office, and a barn, was built in Florida territory in the mid-1830s during the Seminole Wars "as a measure highly important to the peace and safety of the Country," (quoted from a resolution requesting the building of the arsenal, signed by Acting Governor James D. Westcott, Jr., on January 30, 1832). The arsenal was strategically built in Chattahoochee along the Apalachicola River near the junction of the Flint and Chattahoochee Rivers, with "all the advantages of steamboat navigation to the sea-coast" and along the mail route from St. Augustine to Pensacola.

In 1866 the arsenal was ceded by the United States Government and used for ten years as a state penitentiary. There were ledger entries as early as 1870 showing insane persons were housed in the prison, but not until 1877 was it officially used as a state hospital for the mentally ill, being called the State Asylum and later changed to the Florida Hospital for the Insane.

Treatment at the hospital was primarily custodial care. Unsanitary conditions in the overcrowded old buildings were common. But as awareness of mental illness grew in the twentieth century, more humane and therapeutic treatment was provided. Florida State Hospital, its current name, was the only state treatment center for the mentally ill until 1947 and is still the largest facility in use today.

Circa 1915
Courtesy, Florida State Archives

Chapter 19
Making Cairo Our Home

We had lived in River Junction about seven years now. My wife and I decided that the time had come for us to begin to give serious thought about an education for our children. Lillian Lee had already started to school on her sixth birthday. I had not talked to my railroad agent, Mr. Linton, about the probability of us making a move to some other place. I knew that he would try to discourage this as they had no one to fill my place in the office. Sure enough, when I mentioned it to him, he tried to discourage it, but we had made up our minds that our children's education came first.

I was almost sure that it would be a reduction in salary to make a change because the position I had, being in a joint agency of the four railroads, was much better than one out on the line of just one railroad. We owned our home in River Junction and had spent lots of money on it, but after weighing all of the good things by staying there against the future advantages in the way of education for our children, it was easy for us to make up our minds which course to take.

I told Mr. Linton about our plans, and although he would not fully agree with me, he couldn't deny that we were doing the right thing. So some time afterwards a position bulletin came out to fill a vacancy in the Atlantic Coast Line Railroad office at Cairo, Georgia. I bid on it and by way of seniority I was entitled to the position. Though the salary was only about half as much as the one I had at River Junction, we adjusted ourselves accordingly. I did not have to give up any seniority by leaving the joint office of the four railroads, just lesser pay.

The matter of disposing of our home was next in order because we did not want to leave anything behind. After it was known that we were leaving River Junction and wanted to sell our home, Mr. Colson called on me and asked what I wanted for the house. I told him and he took me up on the price. I told Mr. Colson that it would take me a few weeks to get a house in Cairo and move my family. He agreed for them to stay as long as they wanted to. We had a nice jersey cow, Old Pet, that my wife's father had given to her that we sold to the Florida State Hospital. And that wound up all the details except moving, which we would do as soon as I could find a house in Cairo.

I caught an Atlantic Coast Line train for Cairo, arriving there about 1:30 A.M. that night, and on alighting from the train, I came in contact with Mr. Hugh Cannon, who directed me to the Central Hotel. Mr. Cannon asked me if I had a family and I told him that I had a wife and three small children. He invited me to attend services at the First Baptist Church, which we later did. Mr. Cannon was a deacon in the church and was very nice to assist me in every way that he could.

The following day I went out looking for a house. I found them to be very scarce, but finally found one and rented it. After that I reported at the depot and met Mr. J. C. Thames and his force. I explained to Mr. Thames that I had a family and would have to return to River Junction and move them and our household furniture. He told me to get moved before I started to work.

I returned to River Junction and ordered a boxcar to be placed on the side track. I hired Mr. Williams, who ran a delivery service, to haul everything we had and place it in the boxcar. My wife had most everything packed and ready to go, so it didn't take us long to depart from River Junction. I gave shipping instructions to the railroad office and the car was picked up the following morning along with our family. We rode a mixed train [a train carrying both freight and passengers] from River Junction to Climax, Georgia, and changed to Number 58, arriving in Cairo at 1:30 A.M. The night operator, Mr. Godwin, who boarded with Mrs. Yancy Bryan on First Avenue NE, took us to Mrs. Bryan's boardinghouse, and we obtained lodging for the night. We stayed with Mrs. Bryan for several days, until we had our furniture hauled from the boxcar to the home on the north side of Cairo.

Cairo only had one school at that time and it was on the south side, a distance of about one mile from where we lived. Our little girl, as

Life as a Railroad Man

young as she was and in the second grade, walked to school with Mr. Alton Mixon's children—Gladys, Aris, and James. It was my understanding that Doris and Ralph Mixon were not of school age at that time. We soon found out that it was too far for Lillian Lee to walk to school, so we rented what was called the Copeland house on Decatur Street, close to the school. Mr. Haddock was superintendent of schools and Miss Zant was Lillian Lee's teacher.

It was November 5, 1924, when I arrived in Cairo and we had not lived there long before Mr. Linton and Mr. C. L. Moore came from River Junction to talk to me about moving back to River Junction. They claimed that they could not find a man within the Montgomery district of the Atlantic Coast Line that understood freight rates as I did. They also told me that I would be relieved of some of the work that I had done in the past. The relief of some of the work was used as an inducement to take the job back and return to River Junction. But moving back was out of the question with us, so I had to tell them that I was pleased with the work that I was doing and could not accept their offer.

Before moving to Cairo, I was told by Mr. J. P. Linton what a nice small town it was. Mr. Linton's home was in Pavo and his uncle, Mr. J. C. Matthews, was living in Cairo. When Mr. Linton was telling me about the town, he had no idea that someday I would be living there. I recall someone telling me that the population of Cairo was about eighteen hundred in 1924.

As I looked around, I noticed that only a short distance of Broad Street was paved with brick—the rest was hard clay, and when it rained it was slick and mushy. There were no electric street lights, except on the corner of First Avenue and Broad by the Higdon building, which has since been torn down since broadening the avenue. There were several lamps at various places on Broad Street. I do not know what kind of fuel the lamps burned, but I did notice the city's only policeman lighted them with a torch on the end of a stick. The lights were on metal poles not much higher than your head.

I observed water troughs and hitching posts at various places on Broad Street for watering stock and hitching. I never saw such a sight, and never will I again, I am afraid. All of Broad Street was, at times,

Broad Street, Cairo—1916

Cairo's citizens were extremely proud of their lighted street, referred to as the "White Way." Courtesy, Georgia Department of Archives and History.

blocked with a yoke of oxen or horse teams drawing wagons loaded with barrel syrup or bales of cotton. Most of the farmers' products were bought locally by W. B. Roddenbery Company or by the Cane Growers Cooperative Association.

The Cairo policeman was named Mr. Jefferies, and he and family lived in the Beall home on Decatur Avenue and next to our house. The Gus Booths also lived near us on Second Street SE. Our other neighbors were the Weathers, the Kedar Powells, the Dr. T. J. Arlines, the George Hardys, the Bob Wights, and the J. B. Wights. The Haddocks lived on the corner of the school lot. The high school and the grammar school were both in the same building—Mr. Haddock was the principal.

There was only a weekly newspaper in town, The *Cairo Messenger*—Mr. H. H. Wind was editor. The city had its own light plant and one water tank. They collected a four dollar street tax, and if you couldn't pay it when due, you could work it out at the rate of one dollar per day. The city also sold home-made sanitary toilets.

Within the city limits, there were three churches—the Baptist, Methodist, and Presbyterian. There were three banks here—Cairo Banking Company, Citizens Bank, and Farmers' and Merchants' Bank, all on South Broad Street. The post office was located across the alley from the City Hall—Mr. Crawford was the postmaster.

There were two horse and mule stables in town. One was on First Avenue SW and operated by Mr. J. W. Crapps. The other was on First Avenue NE and located where the Nicholson Seed and Fertilizer Company is at present and owned by Mr. R. L. Nicholson.

Mr. Dyson operated a casket shop and factory located near the Atlantic Coast Line tracks about where the Joseph Campbell Company's plant is now. The old Central Hotel, Cairo's only hotel and where I spent my first night, was operated by G. D. Reddick. It was located near the courthouse. Cairo did not have but one furniture store, Cairo Furniture Company, and it was owned and operated by Mr. B. W. Mauldin.

There was a hospital on the corner of South Broad Street and Second Avenue, owned and operated by Dr. W. A. Walker. Other

Atlantic Coast Line Railroad Depot, Cairo—Circa 1916

A lone horse-drawn wagon waits to pick up freight at the Cairo, Georgia, railroad depot. Wight Hardware Store can be seen in the group of buildings lining South Broad Street. Courtesy, Georgia Department of Archives and History.

Life as a Railroad Man

doctors in town were Dr. T. J. Arline, Dr. Lindsey, and Dr. Warnell. Dr. Walker later built the brick hospital on Second Avenue SE.

There were two dentists in town when we moved there—Dr. W. M. Searcy and Dr. T. J. Butt. Dr. H. L. Cheney came later. Mr. W. M. Searcy, Sr. had Monticello coal shipped in, and it did not take long for him to dispose of a carload as there were no other fuels except wood. Thomas-Robinson Lumber Company located here later and fuel wood was more plentiful, but coal was mostly used.

There were three drug stores—the two on South Broad Street were Wight & Brown and Grady Pharmacy. The Central Drug Store was in the Roddenbery Building just north of the railroad. The two hardware stores were the Wight Hardware on South Broad Street and Roddenbery Hardware Company on North Broad Street.

Mr. Hugh Cannon operated a syrup barrel factory in one of the buildings where W. H. Robinson, Inc. was later located. Mr. Tom Bartlett was the barrel cooper. As I remember, the telephone office was upstairs in the J. R. White Grocery building—Miss Tessie Mott was the telephone operator. There were no chain stores or supermarkets in Cairo and the independent stores fought vigorously to keep them out. There were three wholesale grocery stores—Ira Higdon Grocery, Collins Wholesale Grocery, and Montgomery Wholesale Grocery. Fifty years later, you should see Cairo—lots of industries and over ten thousand inhabitants.

Mr. Sam Pierce organized a band. I had already been in two bands playing the coronet, so I joined it. The city built us a bandstand in Davis Park and we gave Sunday afternoon concerts. We often gave concerts from the space on top of the small building now operated by Barbara's Beauty Salon on First Avenue SW. At times we would march and play from Broad Street to the Triangle.

The warehouse we had at the Atlantic Coast Line Railroad was always filled from end to end, and sometimes we had to have boxcars placed at the platform to take care of the overflow. Peanuts at that time were not considered one of the principal crops as they are today. Collard seed was one of the money crops for the farmers. The first freight shipment that I billed out at the station was a carload of collard

Walker H. Reddick, Sr. and Homer—Circa 1929
Courtesy, Anne and W. Homer Reddick, Jr.

Life as a Railroad Man

seed shipped by W. H. Robinson. I thought that this might be enough collard seed to plant the whole world.

In later years a disease almost destroyed the cane, and this disease was fought with every means that the farmers and the U.S. government could muster. They came up with another variety—the stalk was much smaller but made very good syrup. I believe the name of this new cane was kiana—if it's not spelled right I stand corrected. Later, the U.S. government took a hand in improving the agricultural program in Grady County, and they built and equipped a building just north of the W. B. Roddenbery large cane mill north of Cairo. I was told that the price of sugar over the nation was based on the Grady County cane crop.

The largest shippers of syrup were W. B. Roddenbery Company, Robinson Syrup Company, and Cane Growers Cooperative Association. The largest cotton shippers were Wight Hardware Company and Mr. J. M. Paulk. Several others shipped less than a carload. There was a cotton gin here also—it was operated by Mr. G. D. Reddick.

When I started to work in the Atlantic Coast Line Railroad station, Mr. J. C. Thames was the agent and A. A. Mixon was the operator. Other employees were R. L. Williams and D. Godwin. Hugh Lane Lawson had resigned and I took his place as chief clerk and rate clerk. Mr. Thames also had an express clerk. At that time express business was heavy. There were no trucks or buses to handle any of the business so the railroads were loaded to their capacity.

The Pelham and Havana Railroad was still in operation when we moved there. The P and H, as it was called, had physical connections with the Atlantic Coast Line and handled freight and passengers until the Kelley-Clark Lumber Company at Gradyville, south of Cairo, had cut all the available timber and the sawmill closed down. A short time later the P and H also discontinued operation and all of the rail was taken up, cut up, and shipped to Jacksonville for scrap iron.

There weren't many automobiles then, just a few Model Ts, and not many people were financially able to own one, plus the public roads were not paved. Therefore, most of the travel was done by railroad. The Atlantic Coast Line Railroad operated a train from Thomasville,

Georgia, to Bainbridge and later extended to Dothan, Alabama. This train was called the Thomasville to Bainbridge Short [a short line is a railroad with less than one hundred miles of mainline track]. It would make the round trip each day. During the summer months, the churches would get together and charter a train to take a crowd of young people to Valdosta, Georgia, in the morning and return in the afternoon. They would take picnic lunches and go out to Blue Springs, not far from Valdosta, and enjoy bathing in the large pool.

Mr. A. A. Mixon, one of the telegraph operators in the railroad office, would take his family and mine out to Lake Amonia for a fish fry. There was an elderly colored woman who lived near the lake and was most always available to cook all the fish we could eat, along with plenty of the knobies [sometimes called doorknobs, a fried cornmeal batter similar to hushpuppies].

The railroad employees were allowed a vacation each year. If we traveled over any railroad other than the Coast Line, we'd have to make requisition for a "foreign pass" which would take about two weeks. We'd been living in Cairo about two years when I asked for our vacation time for a trip out in Louisiana and Texas. The railroads did not have very comfortable cars then—no screens in the windows and the cinders from the locomotive kept us smutty and uncomfortable all the time. There was not any such thing as air-conditioning then, but we still enjoyed our vacations.

Chapter 20
Days of the Depression

In 1926 the operators struck on the Atlantic Coast Line and the jobs were filled with all kinds of people who were not capable of operating railroads. For some time trains were late and many wrecks occurred with lots of damage to people and property.

The pinch of inflation had its effect on all the people of the United States and business was beginning to slump. These hard times were called the "panic" with thousands of people out of work. Negroes were buying tickets for points up North looking for jobs. Presidents Harding and Coolidge were being blamed for some of this panic, and the 1928 election for president was soon coming up. When it did, Herbert Hoover was nominated to run on the Republican ticket and was elected. Times were so bad that no one had confidence in anyone any more, so he only served one term.

Our railroad superintendent, Mr. Jim Bowdoin, advised me that my job in the office would be discontinued. The word found its way to the business people in Cairo, and Mr. J. M. Hughes, manager of the Chamber of Commerce, circulated a petition which was signed by every businessman in Cairo and forwarded it to Mr. Bowdoin in Montgomery. The petition was urging the superintendent to keep me on in the Atlantic Coast Line office and stressed the fact that it would be better for the Atlantic Coast Line and all concerned to not discontinue my position. Mr. Bowdoin's answer was that he appreciated the interest they had expressed, but if business on the railroad got worse, he would be compelled to abolish the job.

And he did several months later when he came down and talked to me about going to Ozark, Alabama, where my experience in handling remilling-in-transit of lumber was needed. The Ewell Lumber Company at Ewell, about three miles from Ozark, was having timber shipped into their mill from the East and remilled at Ewell and the end product reshipped out to points west. Mr. Bowdoin explained that no one else in his district knew anything about remilling-in-transit rates except me. I told Mr. Bowdoin that he could abolish my job at Cairo if he had to, but hoped that procedure wasn't done to force me to go to Ozark. I made it clear that if and when the job was reestablished at Cairo, I would bid on it and move back to Cairo.

We moved to Ozark, and I was carried down the road to Ewell each day to check on the stock of logs and lumber the Ewell Lumber Company had received and what they had shipped out. When I had finished my first report, I took it to Montgomery and had the Southern Weighing and Inspection Bureau check it and they said it was okay. I taught one of Mr. Pouncy's clerks in his office how to make the reports, and after two weeks a bulletin came out that stated my position in Cairo had been reestablished. I immediately bid on it and we moved back to Cairo into the same house we had moved from. The telephone had not even been removed. The task at Ozark had been completed and we were happy and so was Superintendent Bowdoin.

At this point living conditions were getting intolerable. Money was hard to get and banks all over the country were closing their doors. In this year of 1929 the stock market collapsed and things in general were in a state of confusion. The farmers got very little for their products. Eggs were selling for ten cents per dozen, syrup for twenty cents per gallon. You could buy a nice fryer chicken for fifteen cents and prices of other farmers' products were proportionate.

When the farmers' equipment became worn out, such as wagons, he would get a set of Model T wheels and attach a pair of shafts or a tongue to the two wheels and use an ox, mule, or horse to haul his products to town. They called this new vehicle a Hoover cart. They were generally used and were around for several years.

Finally, when Mr. Franklin Delano Roosevelt was elected president in 1932, things began to look brighter. His first act was to close the doors of all the banks and keep them closed until legislation could be passed on a bill that would guarantee depositors up to twenty thousand

Franklin Delano Roosevelt—1933

FDR visits Florida prior to his first inauguration, riding in a car with Florida Governor Dave Sholtz. Courtesy, Florida State Archives.

Circa 1934. Marion, Homer, and Lillian Lee, "...three of the sweetest children that any couple could wish to have." Courtesy, Anne and W. Homer Reddick, Jr.

Life as a Railroad Man

dollars on all deposits. The banks then started to reopen their doors in 1933, and normal conditions began to come back. The stock market also opened up for business. It seemed that President Roosevelt had put the nation back onto its feet.

During those days of depression, the railroads were feeling the absence of business, and they had cut employees to just barely operate passenger and freight trains. The employees were on a seniority list in each district, and in the Montgomery district I was second on the list in order of seniority. My job was abolished as of April 1, 1933, and there was only one person that I could roll and that was an ex-agency supervisor at River Junction.

The ex-agency supervisor had already been cut and had rolled another man that held the joint accountant's job. And as he carried the title to his former job as agency supervisor, it would be difficult to roll him and stay in good grace with the freight agent there. I went to River Junction with the purpose of feeling out what would happen should I roll this so-called official. The reader should understand that I was fully within my rights in rolling this man, but the trouble would be that the railroad officials together with the agent and this so-called official would stand together.

Since I had worked in the same office with all the other employees for seven years prior to moving to Cairo, I found all of them anxious for me to roll him and get him out of the way. They didn't like him because he was a snooper. The agent tried to be neutral, but I could tell that he had a dislike for me for leaving the force there when I moved to Cairo. I returned to Cairo and told my wife that I didn't have any other place to go or to roll, that I was entitled to the accountant's job at River Junction, and had made up my mind that I would roll Snooper. I notified the superintendent that I was exercising my seniority and would displace the man in the accountant's job.

I went to work on the job and the snooper took the night janitor's job, and I soon found out that he and the agent were keeping in close touch with my work. I had the full cooperation of all the force in the office and they knew that the snooper took the night porter's job so he could look into everything I was doing. Before my wife and children moved to River Junction, the superintendent was down there one day talking to me, and in one of his remarks I realized he knew the contents of one of my wife's letters. The mail came over from the post office at night and it gave Snooper a good chance to open my mail. This made me furious so I went to the post office and had my mail held until I called for it.

I didn't want the job to begin with, and would not have taken it under any other circumstances. This unsatisfactory strain on me and my family made us wish that some other place would come open so we could move.

The superintendent was in River Junction one day, and I asked him if he was going to have another opening soon in the district. He said he was reinstating the job that was cut in Bainbridge, and if I wanted to make a change, I could bid on it. It came open several weeks later. I got the job and we moved to Bainbridge—I think this was in 1934.

Both our daughters, Lillian Lee and Marion Elizabeth, graduated from high school while we lived in Bainbridge, with Lillian Lee entering Georgia State Teacher's College in Statesboro, Georgia.

My wife's father, Mr. M. F. Anderson, passed away in Samson on July 26, 1936. Lillian was made executrix in his last will and testament. After his death we were required to make many trips to points in Alabama in order to execute his will. It so happened that while we lived in River Junction this last time we bought a Model A Ford car which helped us out in our travels over in Alabama in connection with the execution of Lillian's father's will.

We lived in Bainbridge until 1937, when my old job at Cairo came open. I was the successful bidder and we moved back to Cairo with Marion Elizabeth entering South Georgia College at Douglas. We moved into the Latimer house on First Street SW. Lillian Lee and Mr. Carl T. Collins were married in this home by Reverend Wilburn Smith on June 19, 1939.

Mr. Richard Sawyer was station agent when we moved to Cairo and Mr. J. C. Thames, the former agent, had been moved to the Valdosta agency. Mr. Olin Preston was one of the new operators in the Atlantic Coast Line office.

About this time FDR pushed for the passage of a social security bill by Congress, which was to assist elderly people that had retired after

Daughter
Lillian Reddick Collins

Son-in-law
Carl T. Collins, Sr.

Grandson
Carl T. Collins, Jr.

Granddaughter
Sylvia J. Collins

Grandson
Stephen F. Collins

Photos provided by the author.

sixty-five years of age to exist in a meagerly way. This act of Congress made way for modern social security to be financed by the employee paying in so much and the employer matching the employee's amount. This was to increase by a small percentage each year. This social security went into effect in the mid-1930s, and from the standpoint of the elderly people, this was the most important piece of legislation passed by the Congress in many years. President Roosevelt was given the credit for having the bill introduced. The Congress business began to pick up and the panic of the past had about disappeared. Prosperity was in the making.

In 1940, Roosevelt was reelected for the third time. About a year later, my wife and I, on a Sunday afternoon, had been out for a walk in the cemetery. When we returned home we found our daughter, Marion, and her friend, Maribob Forrester, almost glued to the radio. They immediately told us that Japan had bombed Pearl Harbor, several of our battleships had been destroyed, and over two thousand of our navy and military men had been killed. We joined them by the radio and the news by that time had spread all over the nation—the air was full of it.

The next day we heard President Franklin Delano Roosevelt calling both houses of Congress in session for the purpose in declaring war on Japan. I remember his words to the Congress: "I ask that the Congress declare, that since the unprovoked and dastardly attack by Japan on Sunday, December 7, 1941, a state of war has existed between the United States and the Japanese Empire." War was immediately declared, and with all haste that could be put forth, men were being drafted for the Army and Navy. Ships were being built for convoying troops across the ocean. Germany was already at war with France, Great Britain, and Russia. Now we were in the war.

All men of certain ages were ordered to register for service. I registered but was too old to serve. Extra trains were being run loaded with troops to points of embarkation. And food stamps came into existence. I think we have some of the food stamps now as keepsakes.

President Roosevelt did not live to see us win the war—when he died we lost one of the best presidents this nation has ever known. He died in Warm Springs, Georgia, and Vice President Harry Truman was sworn in as president. It was he that had to make the most important decision of any president this nation has ever had, to give orders for the atomic bomb to be dropped on Japan, which was accomplished with much success. This caused the surrender of the Japanese Army and Navy. And soon thereafter, our allies closed in on Germany, and General Eisenhower with all his military skill together with Great Britain's assistance, landed thousands of troops on Normandy. And this was the end of the war.

Daughter
Marion Reddick Watson
Photo provided by the author.

Marion Elizabeth and Mr. Don Watson were married on October 6, 1945, in Lee Baptist Church in Valdosta. Our only son, Walker Homer, attended Gordon Lee Academy at Chickamaugua, Georgia, later Norman Junior College, Norman Park, Georgia, and went on to Florida State University, Tallahassee, where he received his masters degree.

Chapter 21
Attacked by a Cock-Fighting Rooster

During the war I had served several years over my required retirement age and gave the Atlantic Coast Line Railroad notice of my resignation effective as early as they could relieve me. In my resignation I informed the superintendent that should he need me, I would return and help out, because I was aware of the fact that the war was still being fought and the railroads needed help. My resignation was accepted, and in just a short time I was called back to work in the Bainbridge office. I knew that this would be only temporary, so I made no preparations to move my family. This was during the winter, and I had to catch a bus, leaving Cairo before daylight and returning on a late afternoon bus.

One morning about ten o'clock after I had begun work in Bainbridge, I was told, "Mr. Reddick, your house is burning up!" We had purchased this home at 415 North Broad Street in May 1942 from Mrs. Ethel Blanton. A bus was scheduled to leave Bainbridge for Cairo in about five minutes. It was closer to the highway where the bus would pass than it was to the bus station, so Mr. Colucke, the agent, rushed me in his car to the highway in time to catch the bus.

When I arrived at our home I could see all our furniture and other belongings scattered over the yard, including Lillian Lee's who was living with us part-time as her husband was serving in the navy. We had a large double garage in the backyard and our neighbors helped us fill it to the top with our household goods.

A man with the Forsyth Insurance Company of Cairo notified the company he worked for in Valdosta, and they had an adjuster, Mr. Leonard, on the spot the following day. Mr. W. M. Tyson, a sawmill man and building contractor and friend of ours, came and made a price for rebuilding the house. Mr. Tyson, Mr. Leonard, and I met in Mr. Forsyth's office. Mr. Leonard was very reasonable in assessing his estimated loss and damage to our clothing and furniture, and in addition, he allowed us several hundred dollars in case some of our belongings were missing. Mr. Tyson and I agreed on the price to rebuild the house. My wife and I stayed with Misses Tessie and Velma Mott until our house was rebuilt. We could not have found a better place to stay.

It was not long after our house caught fire and the repairs were made that I left the Atlantic Coast Line Railroad again and accepted bookkeeping jobs for wholesale grocery stores in Cairo. But after several months, I realized I still had railroading in my system and my desires led me to the point where my mind was made up to try it again, but not with the Atlantic Coast Line Railroad this time. I wrote Mr. White, the superintendent of the Georgia and Florida Railroad in Augusta, Georgia, to see if he had a vacancy for agency/operator, and if so to consider my application.

I immediately received a telegram from Mr. White to report to his office in Augusta. I did, and he told me to take over the agency at Edgefield, South Carolina, which was only a few miles from Augusta. Mr. Idus Jones, the former agent, suffered a stroke and could no longer telegraph so I was checked in as agent. The Georgia and Florida Railroad had discontinued handling passengers on their line from Augusta to Greenwood, South Carolina, so I didn't have any tickets to sell and had two large waiting rooms that were empty. I secured board and lodging at Mrs. Reel's Tourist Home just up the hill from the station. My wife joined me a few months later and we purchased a Hot Spot electric stove and improvised one of the waiting rooms for our kitchen and continued to occupy the room at Mrs. Reel's.

I handled all the carload and less than carload freight, express, and Western Union Telegraphing. I had one competitor, the Southern Railroad. I soon met the agent, Mr. Anderson, and we became friends, so I did not have much trouble in getting the Georgia and Florida Railroad share of the business in and out of Edgefield.

Lillian and I were fond of Edgefield for it was a very nice town. It was the seat of government for Edgefield County and included the homes of some distinguished members of Congress. Lots of people came there to attend court and conduct other government business. Edgefield was on the main highway from the north to Charleston and Myrtle Beach, coast towns on the Atlantic, so many tourists stopped there. The main industry was a large textile mill that employed many workers. They also had a nice hotel there in addition to Mrs. Reel's Tourist Home.

We also learned that the birthplace of a very distinguished and beloved Baptist minister, Dr. R. G. Lee, was just a short distance from Edgefield. At our first opportunity we attended the First Baptist Church and presented our letters for membership. The minister was Reverend John Wimbash. The membership of this church was about four hundred. At prayer service on Wednesday nights, almost all the membership attended, including all the deacons of the church. We found ourselves among one of the loveliest groups of people we had ever met.

During a revival, Dr. R. G. Lee was the visiting preacher. I was on a committee to see that all visiting people's cars were properly parked to give room for all, and we, the committee, checked license tags on cars from five different states. There were so many for baptism that Dr. Lee had some kind of rack made.

South Carolina has the distinction of having more cock-fighting roosters than any other state in the union, and it is legal there. Before my wife came from Cairo to join me, I left the station to go uptown, and I went a different way other than my regular route. About half way I encountered one of those South Carolina long-spurred monsters, and he was all over my back before I realized what had happened. I had noticed this rooster and several hens off to one side, but I thought nothing about it until I was attacked. He did not pierce me with his spurs as I didn't give him time because I was fighting to get rid of him. Afterwards I took the other route to town.

But this same old rooster and his girlfriends, the hens, did their courting and scratching near the depot. I was handling much grain feed through the warehouse and some sacks would lose some on the floor.

It occurred to me that I could get back on this game-cock, so I scattered some of the grain outside the depot to get him into the warehouse, which one day I succeeded in doing. I closed the doors and had him all to myself. There were some gall bushes growing close to the depot and I cut several switches and was now ready for revenge.

He soon realized that he had no way of escape, so he started to put up a bluff. When he came at me, I let him have it with the two switches and beat him just as much as he would have liked to beat me. When I opened the warehouse door he flew out, as bloody as he was, and ran to be with his flock of hens. This old rooster avoided me the rest of the time I was in Edgefield, and I could go to town any route I wished without fear of being attacked by him. I probably should not write about this incident, but when it came to my mind, I could not resist.

The ladies of Edgefield took my wife on a tour of the beautiful colonial homes of the city and countryside. My wife reported that they were indeed beautiful. We also had the opportunity of visiting nearby towns, including the capital city of Columbia, and we saw the large peach groves of that section of the state.

We were in Edgefield for about one year when the superintendent wanted me to take the Adel, Georgia, agency. As much as we loved Edgefield, we wanted to be closer to our home, so we decided to accept the agency at Adel.

We found Adel, like Edgefield, a very nice town. The former agent of the Georgia and Florida Railroad there had a heart attack—he could no longer keep the agency and had to retire. The work was similar to that at Edgefield except there was much more work involved. At Adel I had the express agency in addition to other work for the railroad, and the Southern Railroad competition was much more competitive.

The largest commodities shipped out from Adel were tobacco and pickles. The large pickle plant was near my station, and I had to keep the plant furnished with cars to ship their product out. The Southern Railway also solicited its shipments, as both railroads had physical rail connections. But the Georgia and Florida Railroad, which I represented, had the advantage on securing a larger portion of the tobacco shipments outbound. We had several rooms built on to the main office building especially for offices for the tobacco buyers, and, of course, they would ship their tobacco over the Georgia and Florida Railroad. The Southern Railway kept a soliciting agent in Adel on full time, and neither he nor their freight agent was as cooperative as I found the agent of the Southern at Edgefield.

I did not own a truck to deliver the express shipments, and it was necessary that I rent the truck that the former agent used. Also I had two young men on the delivery truck who were not responsible, and one of them was supposed to be my clerk in the office, but both stayed out on the truck most of the time. The office work was heavy, but I managed to keep it going until one day I was trying to check the express that was piled to the ceiling when I was pulling down some boxes. One large box fell on my foot and broke two of my toes. I continued to work, though, with a bedroom slipper on that foot, but finally I had to go to a doctor and have the toes bandaged. The doctor advised me to not bear any weight on that foot until it was entirely well. This was discouraging to me, and without sufficient help, I decided that I would resign.

I wired in my resignation to the Georgia and Florida Railroad and also to the Railway Express Agency. It was two weeks before I was relieved. We had put our letters in the First Baptist Church in Adel, and for the short time we were there, we had gained many good friends. My age at this time was fifty-eight.

Chapter 22
Visit to the Old Home Place

We returned to Cairo and while our house was being vacated by renters, we decided to visit our daughter Lillian and her husband, Carl Collins, in Newman, Georgia. While we were there, I had a telephone call from Mr. B. W. Mauldin advising me that Mr. Wyman H. Richter wanted a bookkeeper and said I could have the job if I would return soon. We immediately returned to Cairo, and I started to work as bookkeeper with Mr. Richter in the wholesale vegetable and pecan business.

This business bought vegetables on the state market and trucked them to the state market in Atlanta. They had their own processing plant for grading and polishing pecans and shipping them out to many customers in several states in carload and less than carload shipments. I continued working with Mr. Richter for about two years, and my tenure there was perfectly gratifying to me as I found Mr. Wyman Richter a very agreeable person to work for. At this time I was sixty years old. During this time our son Walter Homer and Miss Anne Hardwick were married on September 4, 1947.

The mayor and council of the City of Cairo appointed me city clerk and treasurer in 1950, following the resignation of Mr. Ralph Carlisle. I held this position until the later part of 1955, when I reached the age of sixty-five and could take my railroad retirement and social security.

On my resignation, I was immediately appointed by the Grady County Hospital Board as manager and bookkeeper. After I had started on the job, I found that the hospital was badly in arrears in paying their bills and meeting their payrolls. With the assistance of the hospital auditor, we put in a new system of bookkeeping and patient admittance

Son
W. Homer Reddick, Jr.

Daughter-in-law
Anne H. Reddick

Grandson
Walker H. Reddick

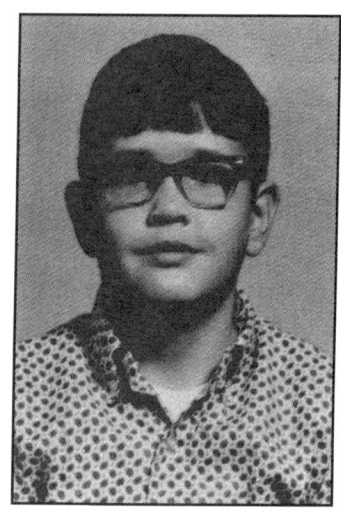

Grandson
Hardwick Anderson Reddick

Photos provided by the author.

| Life as a Railroad Man | 165 |

rules. The board also gave me some assistance by acquiring Mr. Willie Strickland as office assistant. I served in this position for about two years, and when I resigned, all bills had been paid and all discounts taken, leaving over ten thousand dollars in the checking account. After I left the hospital, I kept books for Brown Tractor Company in Cairo until they went out of business.

Let me relate what I decided to do with my spare time since I was over sixty-five and had put in thirty-seven years of almost continuous service with the six different railroads. And if you have read all of this life's history, you can readily see that there hasn't been any time for idleness. I had for many years tried to make something important and useful that I might have patented. I did not have in mind that I would bring in a million dollars, not at all, but just to make something useful. No one knows how long he or she will live on this earth, but I had in mind that I would have about twenty years left and that might be long enough for me to accomplish what I had wished to do.

I didn't have any tools, but I wanted to build a shop in my backyard and just build things. Before I left the Atlantic Coast Line Railroad, I made what I called a rate box—not many people except myself know what a rate box is—but I made it and have the old thing among some other complicated contraptions in my possession. It was a time saver, so much so that our superintendent noticed me using it and wanted me to take it to the headquarters in Wilmington, North Carolina, and have it patented. But I didn't take it because I made it for my own use and did not care to let any one else steal my idea. I continued using it, however. I made many other useful things that I put aside, and later I saw where someone else had made one of them and patented it.

When we moved into this house that we have now lived in for thirty-four years, there was a large wooden frame double garage in our backyard. I tore the garage down and used the material to make me a long shelter with plenty of room to keep materials in. And there was a small smokehouse in the backyard too, and Homer helped me shift the building using iron pipe rollers to one corner of our lot, connecting it with the shelter that I had made. I used this room for a tool house.

The only tools that I had at that time were one hand saw, one brace and bit, one hammer, one plane, and one chisel. With these tools I made several fishing skiffs for use in the fish ponds in this county. I do not remember how many I built, but I received more orders than I could fill. My son-in-law, Carl Collins, who was business manager for Martha Berry College in Mount Berry, Georgia, gave me a good woodworking machine, which was a big help. I made several pieces of furniture for people. They'd have me come into their homes and take measurements for a particular match piece of furniture, after which I would make the desired item.

I made one boat that Carl and I took up to Mount Berry and sailed it on one of their beautiful lakes, the Victory Lake. I also had a grindrock in my shop and often sharpened knives, garden tools, and scissors. I never made a charge for doing any of these odd jobs.

I was treasurer for the First Baptist Church in Cairo and Mr. Ben Mauldin often helped me do repairs and painting to the church building. I was treasurer for over thirty years and when I resigned in 1965 the church presented me with an award with the following inscription: "Presented to W. H. Reddick in grateful appreciation for faithful service as treasurer of First Baptist Church, Cairo, Georgia." I have enjoyed my work in the First Baptist Church, and have held many important positions. I have been a deacon for fifty-seven years and at this time am an emeritus deacon.

Until two years ago my health had been very good, and I was always busy in my shop, which I enjoyed. My last project was to build a three-wheeled bicycle that I could use to bring our groceries from town, as the grocery men had discontinued making house deliveries. I did lots of work on the thing but I will never finish it as I had some coronary trouble that slowed down most of my energy. I have not given up yet at the age of eighty-seven, because I have obligated myself to assist my wife, who is eighty-six, with the housework.

I can truthfully say that this marriage to Lillian, this fine Christian woman, was the turning point in my life, and I could never have selected another life-mate as honest and faithful. She has been, and still is, the most wonderful person in the world to me. And in these wonderful years together, without any doubt or reservation, she has changed my life from a wandering boy searching for happiness. My wife

May 5, 1976, was the sixtieth wedding anniversary of Walker and Lillian Reddick. "I can truthfully say that this marriage to Lillian...was the turning point in my life, and I could never have selected another life-mate as honest and faithful." Courtesy, Anne and W. Homer Reddick, Jr.

has borne to us three of the sweetest children that any couple could wish to have.

    They are all grown now. Marion Elizabeth, the middle daughter, passed away in Rome, Georgia, in Floyd Hospital on January 23, 1966. Lillian Lee and her husband, Carl Collins, live in Rome and have three grown children, Carl Jr., Sylvia, and Stephen; and three grandchildren. Walker Homer and his wife, Anne Hardwick Reddick, live in Macon, Georgia; and had two boys: Walker Homer is in college at Milledgeville, Georgia, and Hardwick Anderson, the younger, passed away August 1, 1971. This makes my wife and me having three great-grandchildren at this writing. Lillian and I celebrated our sixtieth wedding anniversary on May 5, 1976.

    I shall not close this autobiography without saying something about our good neighbors, not only in Cairo, but in all the places that we have lived. And I can truthfully say that we can claim most every family in Cairo for our neighbors, for all of them have been wonderful to us. To be more personal, I shall name some of them—Mrs. Florence Watts, the Byron White family, Mrs. Roger Matthews Madison, Miss Wessie Connell, Mrs. Ellis, Mrs. Paul Singletary, Mrs. Martha Thomason, Mrs. A. E. Peacock, Mr. and Mrs. D. Y. Hadden, Mrs. G. L. Worthy and her sister Mrs. Beatty, Mrs. Jewel Surles, Mr. and Mrs. Clower White, Mrs. Ruth Campbell, Mr. and Mrs. Ben Mauldin, Mrs. Dadie Paulk, Mr. Louie Powell, and Reverend and Mrs. William Small-Mixon. Also Mrs. Louisa Sheehy, Miss Ann Rooks, Mrs. Beatty Gandy, Miss Clara Mauldin, Mrs. Slater Wight, and the Arline girls, Mr. and Mrs. Hubert Walker, and Mrs. Clarice Singletary. I must say that we love our pastor and his family. We miss them when they are out of town. Brother Franklin is very nice to visit either of us when we are sick—at home or in the hospital.

    I saved the Misses Tessie and Velma Mott until the last as we have always claimed them as our relatives. Anybody that will get up at one or two o'clock in the morning, not one time, but anytime we call, and take either of us to the hospital when we are sick and stay with us until the nurse contacts the doctor and we've been put to bed, is the most precious. But that is not the half of it. They will cook a full meal and bring it to our home and do our shopping. Before bedtime every night

| Life as a Railroad Man | 169 |

the telephone will ring and it is one of the Mott girls asking us if we are all right. This is not a full measurement of the things they do for us, but only a few. Which is why we claim that we are closely related. We thank God for this kind of Christian people.

Three of my nieces, Mrs. Valeta Jernigan Rudio, Mrs. Inita Jernigan Horton, and Mrs. Jean Jernigan Gwinn, took me on a trip to the place where I was born, Point Washington, Florida, last year in 1975. It was late when we arrived there, but we contacted Mrs. Evie Wesley Saltsman, who was a long-time native of Point Washington and was in school at the same time I was. We talked with Evie for awhile and she informed us that the old Wesley home, now Eden State Gardens, was closed for the day.

We drove on out to Grayton Beach and I met some friends I knew in years gone by. I ran into Mrs. [Wilhelmina "known as Bill"] Patterson whose home now is in Pensacola. She is one of the Miller family and we reminisced about the good old days when I spent my vacations at the hotel Aunt Eliza Bowers operated in Grayton and the good times that everyone had. We talked about the people who came from far off to bask in the sun and fish in the beautiful lake there.

My nieces and I traveled on down to Destin where we spent the night and returned to Point Washington the following morning. We visited Eden and Ollie Sue Butler, who was a grand-niece of the builder of the old Wesley mansion and the daughter of Mrs. Evie Wesley Saltsman, the school friend mentioned above.

This same day we visited old Santa Rosa, which was destroyed when canker infested or killed the roots of all the fruit trees and destroyed all the vegetable crop lands, and the people had to leave there or starve. The post office at Santa Rosa was now out on Highway 98 and the road was paved on into the old town. We drove on down there to the bayou and found a large cement foundation for the engine of the McKenzie Lumber Company. Two or three houses were built off the road but there were no signs of people living there. We did find a lady in the office of a mosquito extermination and spraying plant. The lady lived on the west side of Mack Bayou and gave us information about the other families who lived near her home. I have in mind to write a

The Wesley Home Transforms into Eden State Gardens

The Point Washington home of W. H. Wesley, his wife, Katie Strickland Wesley, and their nine children, was built between 1895 and 1897. The 5500-square-foot, two-story home had a central hallway and stairs surrounded by four large rooms, complete with fireplace, on each floor. Seven rooms were used as bedrooms with the eighth serving as a parlor. A separate kitchen, dining room, and storage area were attached in the back.

The dilapidated Wesley home was purchased by Miss Lois Maxon in 1963 for $12,500. She took the old Victorian home and, at the cost of a million dollars, reconstructed it as an 1850 Greek Revival antebellum home. Miss Maxon named her home "Eden," and in 1968 donated the home and gardens to the State of Florida in loving memory of her parents. The author visited the home at Eden State Gardens with his three nieces during his 1975 visit. Photo provided by the author.

full history of this town and when it was no town at all, when I get through with this history of my life.

We continued onto Mack Bayou on the Four Mile Point Peninsula and met several friends there. We spent several hours with Mrs. Alice L. Davis and her son Robert. We were very proud that we saw them, as they were two very lovable people. Robert took his jeep and carried us, all four of us, out to the small Reddick cemetery which was a short distance from their home on the west side of Mack Bayou on Dr. Walker's estate. Robert helped us clear up some of the vines and shrubbery and we obtained the names from the granite slabs which we made a record of. This small burial plot was on my father's land and near the schoolhouse he built.

We also stopped in Fort Walton for a short time, then onto Whitfield where we conversed with Mr. Charlie "Tots" Brown. Then we drove through Freeport on the way to my home in Cairo. I enjoyed every minute of the trip and I am sure that the nieces did too.

Walter H. Reddick, Sr.—August 20, 1975

The author paid his respects to his beloved mother and father at Hatcher Cemetery west of Freeport during his visit to his boyhood home.
Courtesy, Anne and W. Homer Reddick, Jr.

The Four Mile Peninsula was the loveliest place that anyone could wish for. My father and mother could never have selected a better place to raise their family. We had nothing to worry about—we could do as we pleased, go when we wanted to. We never had to plan weeks and months ahead, and when a decision was made, like taking a trip, we just hitched up a team of horses or got into a sailboat and fulfilled that decision. The whole environmental conditions of my childhood were such that my whole life was molded to recreate my success in this world. And this is my life!

FAMILY GENEALOGY

THE REDDICK/O'NEAL FAMILY

HENRY [WILLIAM] REDDICK was born June 16, 1833 and died June 28, 1924. He was buried in Hatcher Cemetery near Portland, Florida.

ELIZABETH G. MCCORMICK was born January 20, 1855 and died January 11, 1924. She was buried in Hatcher Cemetery near Portland, Florida.

[HENRY WILLIAM REDDICK was joined in holy matrimony with ELIZABETH G. MCCORMICK on September 17, 1874.[1]]

THE CHILDREN OF HENRY W. REDDICK BY HIS FIRST WIFE

ELLEN REDDICK was born July 18, 1870 and died January 31, 1959. She was buried in Ernest Grace's plot in the [Riverside[1]] Cemetery in Jacksonville, Florida.

ETTA [LOUISE] REDDICK was born September 6, 1873 and died January 18, 1963 [or 1965[1]]. She is buried in Foxworth Cemetery in Foxworth, Mississippi.

THE CHILDREN OF ELIZABETH G. MCCORMICK BY HER FIRST HUSBAND—SURNAME O'NEAL

WILLIAM A. O'NEAL [known as "Will"] was born August 28, 1871 [and died in 1952[2]]. He was buried in Wright Cemetery in Fort Walton Beach, Florida.

MARCUS LAFAYETTE O'NEAL [known as "Lafayette"] was born August 2, 1872 [or August 8, 1872[1]] and died August 8, 1963. He was buried in [Shadyrest[1]] Cemetery, Holly Hill, Florida.

[All information in brackets has been added by the editor and may not be accurate. See endnotes for sources.]

THE CHILDREN OF HENRY W. REDDICK AND ELIZABETH G. MCCORMICK O'NEAL REDDICK

JEFFERSON MONROE REDDICK was born July 2, 1875 and died September 20, 1885 at the age of ten. He was buried in Reddick Cemetery on Four Mile Point just west of Mack Bayou, now Walton County, Florida.

HENRY TILDEN REDDICK [known as "Tilden"] was born August 8, 1877 and died November 29, 1920. He was buried in Hatcher Cemetery near Portland, Florida.

IDA E. REDDICK was born April 6, 1879 and died March 2, 1965. She was buried in Pinecrest Cemetery in Mobile, Alabama.

ANNIE JEANNETTE REDDICK [known as "Jeannette"] was born on April 11, 1881 and died October 3, 1973. She was buried in Quincy Cemetery in Quincy, Florida.

MILLARD FILMORE REDDICK was born December 10, 1884 [or December 20, 1884[3]] and died June 1, 1891 at the age of six. He was buried in Reddick Cemetery on Four Mile Point just west of Mack Bayou, now Walton County, Florida.

JOHN H. REDDICK was born December 17, 1886 and died December 6, 1974. He was buried in Vernon Cemetery in Vernon, Florida, beside his wife Bama.

WALKER H. REDDICK, SR. was born May 5, 1889 [and died July 14, 1981. He was buried in Greenwood Cemetery in Cairo, Georgia[1]].

GUY REDDICK was born April 1, 1897 and died April 6, 1897. He was buried in Reddick Cemetery on Four Mile Point just west of Mack Bayou, now Walton County, Florida.

THE MARRIAGES OF THE REDDICK/O'NEAL CHILDREN

ELLEN REDDICK was joined in holy matrimony with **CHRIS GRACE**.

ETTA REDDICK was joined in holy matrimony with **GREEN [PATTERSON] MCDONALD** [on February 17, 1891[4]].

WILLIAM A. O'NEAL was joined in holy matrimony with [(first wife) **AMANDA**] and [(second wife) **MARY ANNA HATTAWAY**[2]].

MARCUS LAFAYETTE O'NEAL was joined in holy matrimony with **BELL PIPPIN** [on August 10, 1902[5]].

HENRY TILDEN REDDICK was joined in holy matrimony with **EDNA SENTERFIT** [on July 19, 1905[6]].

IDA E. REDDICK was joined in holy matrimony with (first husband) **CHARLES WESLEY** and (second husband) **CLAUDE WILLIAMS**.

JEANNETTE REDDICK was joined in holy matrimony with **E. H. JERNIGAN** [on February 13, 1901[7]].

JOHN H. REDDICK was joined in holy matrimony with (first wife) **IDA DAVIS** [before 1916] and (second wife) **BAMA WARD** [on May 3, 1919[8]].

WALKER H. REDDICK, SR. was joined in holy matrimony with **LILLIAN LEA ANDERSON** [on May 5, 1916[1]].

THE FAMILIES OF THE REDDICK/O'NEAL CHILDREN

[THE CHILDREN OF ELLEN REDDICK AND HER HUSBAND CHRIS GRACE]

[The author did not list the Grace children. In the text he states the Grace family had six children while living in Point Washington, Florida.]

[THE CHILDREN OF ETTA LOUISE REDDICK AND HER HUSBAND GREEN MCDONALD]

[**VELMA LEILA MCDONALD STUBBS** was born December 24, 1894 and died August 5, 1995.

HENRY MCDONALD was born about 1895.

JOSEPH TILLMAN MCDONALD was born about 1897.

GREEN FRANKLYN MCDONALD was born July 7, 1901 and died October 26, 1965.

SARAH ELIZABETH MCDONALD GRAHAM (known as "Bessie") was born July 14, 1903 and died December 28, 1988.

ETTA LEE MCDONALD SPIERS was born January 15, 1906 and died October 9, 1989.

EVELYN MCDONALD PITTMAN was born July 22, 1914 and died November 12, 1976.[4]]

THE CHILDREN OF WILLIAM A. O'NEAL

By First Wife [AMANDA]

CLYDE O'NEAL, last known address was Bloomsburg, Pennsylvania—deceased.

JOSEPH O'NEAL, Pensacola, Florida—retired.

By Second Wife [MARY ANNA HATTAWAY[2]]

[HENRY] TILDEN O'NEAL, Birmingham, Alabama [was born October 24, 1922 and died August 1999[2]].

[LOIS MARIE O'NEAL CARON, Niceville, Florida, was born April 11, 1925.[2]]

WILLIAM O'NEAL (known as "Bill"), Portland, Florida [was born August 30, 1927[2]].

THE CHILDREN OF MARCUS LAFAYETTE O'NEAL AND HIS WIFE BELL PIPPIN O'NEAL

AVERY O'NEAL, Akron, Ohio—deceased.

NIOMA RHODES O'NEAL, DeFuniak Springs, Florida

RAY O'NEAL, Daytona Beach, Florida—deceased.

ROSS O'NEAL, Daytona Beach and Holly Hill, Florida

EVELYN SMITH O'NEAL, Sanford, Florida

CLYDE RUFFIN O'NEAL, Daytona Beach, Florida

MARIE CARPENTER O'NEAL, Daytona Beach, Florida

THE CHILDREN OF HENRY TILDEN REDDICK AND HIS WIFE EDNA SENTERFIT REDDICK—both deceased

COSTON L. REDDICK, Jacksonville, Florida [died January 21, 1981[1]].

SHELDON REDDICK [was born September 15, 1908 and died October 4, 1919[6]].

STELZIE [T.] REDDICK [was born April 23, 1911 and died October 11, 1969[6]].

THE CHILDREN OF IDA E. REDDICK
AND HER HUSBAND CHARLES WESLEY, Mobile, Alabama—deceased

JEANNETTE WESLEY MCLAURIN, Laurel, Mississippi—deceased. Jeannette had twin daughters who never married.

SHEROD EMANUEL WESLEY, Mobile, Alabama

THE CHILDREN OF JEANNETTE REDDICK
AND HER HUSBAND E. H. JERNIGAN, Quincy, Florida—both deceased

INITA JERNIGAN HORTON, Quincy, Florida [was born September 21, 1901[9] and died July 1994[10]]. (Her husband is Roma E. Horton.)

VALETA JERNIGAN RUDIO, Nokomis, Florida [was born December 24, 1903 and died February 14, 1995[9]]. (Her husband is Carl W. Rudio.)

GLYNN JERNIGAN, Marianna, Florida [was born June 9, 1906[11] and died December 12, 1984[10]].

GUY JERNIGAN—deceased [Died as an infant.]

GAIL BORDEN JERNIGAN, Jacksonville, Florida [was born May 11, 1913[9] and died September 1984[10]].

HELEN JERNIGAN SCIVICQUE, Denham Springs, Louisiana [was born October 11, 1914[11]]. (Her husband is Matt Scivicque.)

JEAN JERNIGAN GWINN, Miami, Florida [was born July 12, 1918[12]]. (Her husband is Mack W. Gwinn.)

THE CHILDREN OF JOHN H. REDDICK
AND HIS WIFE BAMA WARD REDDICK

JUNAWANNA REDDICK, Houston, Texas

JOHNNIE REDDICK, JR., Houston, Texas

MAURICE REDDICK (known as "Terry")

DONALD REDDICK, Houston, Texas

MARY REDDICK (known as "Macy"), Vernon, Florida

REGINAL REDDICK (known as "Reggie"), Houston, Texas

THE CHILDREN OF WALKER H. REDDICK, SR.
AND HIS WIFE LILLIAN ANDERSON REDDICK, [born February 3, 1890[1]], Cairo, Georgia

LILLIAN LEE REDDICK COLLINS, Rome, Georgia [was born September 4, 1917 and died May 3, 1984[1]].

MARION ELIZABETH REDDICK WATSON, Cairo, Georgia [was born August 20, 1919 and died January 23, 1966[1]].

WALKER HOMER REDDICK, JR., Millidgeville, Georgia [was born March 26, 1922[1]].

– END OF REDDICK/O'NEAL FAMILY –

| Family Genealogy |

HENRY W. REDDICK'S SIBLINGS AND THEIR FAMILIES

THE CHILDREN OF JAMES W. REDDICK
[born March 14, 1842 and died January 3, 1922[8] **and his wife** ELIZABETH A. COTTON REDDICK (known as "Lizzie"), born October 8, 1852[8] and died October 10, 1929[7]]

[JAMES M. REDDICK was born in 1869 and died in 1885.[8]]

[MARTHA ADELAIDE REDDICK was born February 13, 1870 and died October 25, 1918.[8]]

RANDAL [HAMPTON] REDDICK, Portland, Florida [was born May 22, 1872 and died July 21, 1940[8]].

[LUE ELLA REDDICK was born around 1874.[8]]

[WILLIAM] CHANDLER [RAYFIELD] REDDICK, Portland, Florida [was born January 14, 1877 and died March 21, 1963[8]].

[MARY FRANCIS REDDICK was born January 1879.[8]]

FANNIE REDDICK, Portland, Florida [was born January 4, 1880 and died December 5, 1964[8]].

[JAMES] ROBBIE REDDICK, Portland, Florida [was born August 8, 1885 and died February 14, 1929[8]].

[VELMA ANNIE REDDICK was born January 30, 1890 and died July 25, 1970.[8]]

[INDIANA REDDICK was born January 18, 1895 and died in 1982.[8]]

[Henry Reddick may have had other siblings: Columbus, Martin, and Mark.]

MADISON REDDICK was killed in the Battle of Chickamauga, Georgia [September 19-20, 1863] during the Civil War. He was buried in Confederate Cemetery, Marietta, Georgia. [Freeport Archival Collection shows Madison's birth around 1842. Their records state that he was wounded in both legs at Murfreesboro, Tennessee, on January 2, 1863, and died six days later after his right leg was amputated by Dr. C. J. Walton, 21st Kentucky.]

THE CHILDREN OF SARAH REDDICK BAKER,
Freeport, Florida—deceased

    IDELL BAKER KNIGHT—deceased.

    SADIE BAKER TERVIN, Freeport, Florida—deceased.

    ESTHER BAKER MCCOLLOUGH, Freeport, Florida—deceased.

    WILLIAM BAKER (known as "Bill"), Pensacola, Florida

THE CHILDREN OF GEORGE [WASHINGTON] REDDICK
[born October 26, 1847 and died November 2, 1930[8]], Portland, Florida

[By first wife—**ROSA BREWER**, date of marriage circa 1870[8]]

    [**NORAH** was born in 1871.[8]]

    MARTIN REDDICK [was born December 1871[8]]—deceased.

    COLUMBUS REDDICK [(known as "Clum") was born in 1873 or 1874[8]]—deceased.

    GEORGEANNA REDDICK [was born December 8, 1874[8] and died April 3, 1922[7]].

[By second wife—**GEORGIANA CRAWFORD**, date of marriage circa 1875[8]]

    [**FLORENCE REDDICK** (known as "Flossie") was born in 1876.[8]]

    ALONZO REDDICK [was born in 1877 or 1879[8]]—deceased.

[By third wife—**CRYRENA BREWER** (known as "Rena"), date of marriage circa 1880[8]]

    WILLIAM [RAY] REDDICK (known as "Will") [was born April 7, 1881[8] and died February 13, 1962[7]].

    BELLE REDDICK [was born July 4, 1882[8] and died June 1958[7]].

JAMES REDDICK (known as "Jim") [was born July 26, 1884[8] and died October 7, 1956[7]].

[**BESSIE REDDICK** was born September 18, 1886.[8]]

LIBBY [DELL] REDDICK [was born January 8, 1889[8] and died July 16, 1962[7]].

[**HENRY WILLIAM REDDICK** was born October 31, 1890.[8]]

[By fourth wife—**NANCY A. TAUNTON**, date of marriage May 16, 1893

ALVA RETTA REDDICK was born May 1894.

SILAS RAY REDDICK was born March 11, 1896.

OSSIE REDDICK was born January 1899.

KENNETH REDDICK was born circa 1902.

DALLAS REDDICK was born circa 1904.[8]]

– END OF HENRY W. REDDICK'S SIBLINGS AND THEIR FAMILIES –

THE MCCORMICK FAMILY

JOHN MCCORMICK and GILLIAH MCCORMICK were married September 2, 1816.

JOHN MCCORMICK JR. and ELIZABETH MCCORMICK were married May 19, 1833.

S. D. MCCORMICK and MARTHA JANE MCCORMICK were married December 1, 1850.

JOHN MCCORMICK was born February 26, 1792.

This being the record of my parents. October 2, 1827 know all that looks at this: I, John McCormick, has [sic] given this Holy Bible to my son, William McCormick.

JOHN MCCORMICK was born April 6, 1879.

WILLIAM MCCORMICK was born March 22, 1818.

JAMES MADISON MCCORMICK was born October 1, 1823.

JOHN DAVIS MCCORMICK was born September 16, 1825.

STEPHEN DECATOR MCCORMICK was born January 30, 1827.

JEREMIAH MCCORMICK was born January 9, 1829.

JAMES MUNROE ALLEN departed this life April 20, 1828. He was born in 1821.

WILLIAM JASPER STAFFORD, cousin of above, was born December 24, 1838.

ELIZABETH MCCORMICK was born October 23, 1790.

JOHN MCCORMICK was born February 26, 1792.

MARTHA JANE MCCORMICK was born the 9th of (month not shown), 1832. This being the record of her parents.

The McCormick family as taken from the family Bible of Mrs. Lee Bowers Scott, DeFuniak Springs, Florida. [Mrs. Lee Bowers Scott was the daughter of Eliza McCormick Bowers, Walker H. Reddick's maternal aunt mentioned in the book.]

| Family Genealogy |

JEFFERSON DAVIS MCCORMICK, deceased October 26, 18— (year not given).

ELLEN WINIE MCCORMICK, deceased July 21, 1889.

JOHN SOLOMON MCCORMICK was born April 6, 1852.

ALFORD JONAH MCCORMICK was born September 10, 1854.

WILLIAM LUCIAN MCCORMICK was born October 25, 1858.

THOMAS STEPHEN MCCORMICK was born June 24, 1861.

WILLIAM HENRY MCCORMICK June 3, 1869 (died in St. Petersburg, Florida).

GENOA MCCORMICK was born March 28, 1871.

GILLIAH MCCORMICK, wife of John McCormick, departed this life March 22, 1831.

JERIMAH MCCORMICK, son of above, departed this life November 9, 1841.

JOHN MCCORMICK, father of Levenniah McCormick and husband of Gilliah McCormick, departed this life September 30, 1857.

JOHN MCCORMICK died November 16, 1864 in Cedar Keys, Florida.

WILLIAM L. MCCORMICK, son of S. D. and Martha Jane McCormick, departed this life November 8, 1859.

THOMAS S. MCCORMICK departed this life December 23, 1864.

STEPHEN D. MCCORMICK departed this life January 5, 1865 in Cedar Keys, Florida.

– THIS CONCLUDES RECORDS TAKEN FROM LEE BOWERS SCOTT'S BIBLE –

[Although Walker H. Reddick, Sr. was not clear on this point, I believe the following five names are McCormick sisters, including Mr. Reddick's mother. In his book Mr. Reddick mentions that his mother's father was William McCormick and that her mother was Emily Skipper McCormick, buried in the Reddick Cemetery.]

ELIZABETH G. MCCORMICK was born January 20, 1855. [Walker Reddick's mother]

VIRGINIA MCCORMICK (No record) Last heard of she lived in New Orleans, Louisiana. [In the 1870 census, Virginia is shown as fifteen years old, making her birth around 1856.]

ELIZA MCCORMICK (No record of birth or death but she was buried in DeFuniak Springs Cemetery, DeFuniak Springs, Walton County, Florida. Her husband, **JAMES W. BOWERS**, was buried in Hatcher Cemetery near Portland, Florida.) [In the 1870 census, Eliza is shown as eight years old, making her birth around 1862.]

LUCY MCCORMICK was born April 1, 1865 and died March 2, 1872. She is buried in Reddick Cemetery on Four Mile Point just west of Mack Bayou, now Walton County, Florida.

GENOA MCCORMICK BOYER was born March 28, 1871 and died in St. Petersburg, Florida.

— THE END OF THE MCCORMICK FAMILY RECORD —

This record of the Reddick, O'Neal, and McCormick families was taken partly from my mother's Bible and the Bible of Mrs. Lee Bowers Scott of DeFuniak Springs, Florida.

Walker H. Reddick, Sr.
Signed. Walker H. Reddick, Sr.
415 N. Broad Street, Cairo, Georgia 31728

REDDICK CEMETERY

"I do not remember the passing of the two older brothers, but I do remember little Guy as I was seven years old. I helped my father make the small casket in which he was buried, and soon after, I built a picket fence around the grave and painted it white." Kim Riegel Photography, Copyright © 1999.

REDDICK CEMETERY

GRAVES IN OLD REDDICK CEMETERY ON FOUR MILE POINT JUST WEST OF MACK BAYOU, NOW WALTON COUNTY, FLORIDA

EMILY (SKIPPER) MCCORMICK, mother of Elizabeth G. McCormick [O'Neal] Reddick, was born October 18, 1835 and died February 13, 1876.

LUCY MCCORMICK, sister of Elizabeth G. McCormick [O'Neal] Reddick, was born April 1, 1865 and died March 2, 1872.

JEFFERSON MONROE REDDICK was born July 2, 1875 and died September 20, 1885.

MILLARD FILMORE REDDICK was born December 10, 1884 [or December 20, 1884[3]] and died June 1, 1891.

GUY REDDICK (infant) was born April 1, 1897 and died April 6, 1897.

ROBERT L. THOMAS was born [July 9,[3]] 1881 and died [September 20,[3]] 1893.

LIZZY DRAY PHYALL was born 1885 [or 1795[7]—as of 2001, the stone is broken and all writing is illegible] and died December 21, 18— (not legible).

One child without slab or any description with small wire fence enclosure.

Upon visiting this cemetery [in 1975] we found a rusty fence, no posts, grown into trees. Vines and shrubs grow all about the cemetery. We did what we could to clear away some of the shrubs and vines but the cemetery is still in need of clearing away the leaves and trees. We were directed to the cemetery by Mr. Robert Davis, who lives on Mack Bayou and near the cemetery. Those with me on the visit were Mrs. Inita [Jernigan] Horton, Quincy, Florida, Mrs. Valeta [Jernigan] Rudio, and Mrs. Jean [Jernigan] Gwinn of Miami, Florida. The property where the cemetery is located (ten acres) is owned by a family of Walkers who live in Anniston, Alabama.

— END OF THE REDDICK CEMETERY —

ENDNOTES

[1] Family Bible. The Bible first belonged to Ida Davis Reddick, first wife of John Reddick. At her death it was given to her mother-in-law, Elizabeth McCormick Reddick. It was then handed down to the author, Walker H. Reddick, Sr. The Bible is now in the possession of W. Homer Reddick, Jr. Most entries listing family births, marriages, and deaths are in Walker H. Reddick, Sr.'s handwriting.

[2] Vickie Caron Lewis, Pensacola, Florida, granddaughter of William A. O'Neal

[3] Inscription on headstone at Reddick Cemetery

[4] Thomas Spiers, Columbia, Mississippi, grandson of Etta Reddick McDonald

[5] Marriage certificate on file at the Washington County, Florida, Courthouse. The newlyweds were listed as "Marcus de Lafayette O'Neil and Josie Belle Pippins."

[6] Inscription on headstone at Hatcher Cemetery

[7] Freeport Archival Collection

[8] Shirley Reddick, Pensacola, Florida, wife of Charles Reddick, great-grandson of James W. Reddick

[9] Carl Rudio, Jr., Venice, Florida, grandson of Jeannette Reddick Jernigan

[10] Carol Scivicque Lamm, granddaughter of Jeannette Reddick Jernigan

[11] Helen Jernigan Scivicque, Denham Springs, Louisiana, daughter of Jeannette Reddick Jernigan

[12] Jean Jernigan Gwinn, Miami, Florida, daughter of Jeannette Reddick Jernigan

SUGGESTED READING

THE FOLLOWING SOURCES have proven to be invaluable to the editor in providing the supplemental historical information included in this volume. The reader may choose to seek out one of these listings to obtain further information about people, places, and events that Mr. Reddick reported on.

Carswell, E. W.
    1986 *Holmesteading: The History of Holmes County, Florida.* One of several Northwest Florida history books written by Carswell, this volume is thorough in its account of the Louisville and Nashville Railroad line that ran through the top of Holmes County and the subsequent harvesting of the timber surrounding it.

Coastal Heritage Preservation Foundation, a branch of the South Walton Three Arts Alliance, Inc., ed. and comp.
    1988 *Historic Grayton Beach (Florida).* A descriptive account of thirty-seven historic homes and businesses, this booklet lists the architectural style, original owners, and date each was built (between 1890 and 1948).

Gunning, James
    1993 "The Port St. Joe Route." *Railfan and Railroad Magazine.* Gunning's July 1993 article on the Port St. Joe Route of the Apalachicola Northern Railroad is informative and concise, with photographs to document one of Florida's railroads, past and present.

Jahoda, Gloria
    1967 *The Other Florida.* This clever account of the lesser-known parts of Florida, mainly the Panhandle region, includes a thorough chapter on Dr. John Gorrie and his ice machine invention.

Suggested Reading

Kalmbach Publishing Co., Waukesha, WI
    2000 *The Historical Guide to North American Railroads.* 2d ed. This book documents the railroads that have vanished after 1930 and were more than fifty miles long. Facts, information, maps, and photographs are included on the Louisville and Nashville Railroad, Central of Georgia Railway, and Georgia and Florida Railroad mentioned in Reddick's book.

McKinnon, John L.
    1968 *History of Walton County.* 2d ed. In this formal account of the early life of Walton County pioneers, the author vividly recounts his war-time experience in Company E, Florida First Infantry, of the Walton Guards, Confederate States of America. When this book was written in 1911, Walton County did not contain the land south of the Choctawhatchee Bay.

Mettee, Vivian Foster., et al.
    1970 *...And the Roots Run Deep.* This short-story history of Destin, Florida, includes the neighboring community of Santa Rosa Plantation.

Morris, Allen C.
    1974 *Florida Place Names.* An informative book giving the history behind some of Florida's towns, it contains specific information on St. Joseph and Point Washington.

Price, Richard E.
    1966 *Atlantic Coast Line Railroad: Steam Locomotives, Ships, and History.* An excellent resource book about the history of smaller railroads that were absorbed by larger ones, this book contains excellent photographs and information.

    1969 *Seaboard Airlines Railroad: Steam Boats, Locomotives, and History.*

Reddick, Henry William
    1999 *Seventy-Seven Years in Dixie: The Boys in Gray of '61 - '65.* rev. ed. Originally self-published by the author in 1910, this memoir offers a first-person glimpse into the life of a second lieutenant in Company E, Florida First Infantry, of the Walton Guards, Confederate States of America.

Rogers, William Warren
    1986 *Outposts on the Gulf.* This thoroughly researched account of Apalachicola and St. George Island, Florida, covers the early exploration of the area to events of World War II, including the colorful land developer, William Lee Popham.

South Walton Three Arts Alliance, Inc., ed. and comp.
    1996 *The Way We Were: Recollections of South Walton (County, Florida) Pioneers.* An assortment of recollections from local old-timers about Santa Rosa Plantation, Point Washington, Grayton Beach, and other communities south of the Choctawhatchee Bay in Walton County, Florida, is assembled in this volume.

    1999 *Of Days Gone By: Reflections of South Walton County, Florida.* This collection contains folksy stories about Freeport, Portland, and other towns north of the Choctawhatchee Bay, as well as towns between the Bay and the Gulf of Mexico.

Wells, Anna Paget, and Geraldine Kryder Clemmons
    1980 *Heart and History of Holmes County (Florida) with Glimpses of the Panhandle.* This homespun account of life in Chipley, Noma, and other towns in Holmes County, Florida, includes lists of all the postmasters and the impact both the lumber industry and the Louisville and Nashville Railroad had on the county.

Wells, William James
    1976 *Pioneering in the Panhandle.* A look at selected events and families as a part of the history of South Santa Rosa County, Florida, this book also includes chapters on the lumber industry, General William Miller, and Company E, Florida First Infantry, of the Walton Guards, Confederate States of America.

West, George Mortimer
    1922 *"Old St. Jo" and a Night on a Florida Beach.* A little-known book written by the founder of Panama City, Florida, it recounts the history of Port St. Joe and how yellow fever and hurricanes destroyed old St. Joseph.